T3-BOF-556

CHILDREN OF POVERTY

Studies on the Effects of Single Parenthood, the Feminization of Poverty, and Homelessness

edited by

STUART BRUCHEY
University of Maine

A GARLAND SERIES

CHILD, PARENT OR BOTH?

Who Should be the Focus of an Effective Parenting Program

REBECCA WILLIAMS

GARLAND PUBLISHING, Inc.
New York & London / 1995

Library of Congress Cataloging-in-Publication Data

Williams, Rebecca, 1943–
Child, parent, or both? : who should be the focus of an effective parenting program? / Rebecca Williams.
p. cm. — (Children of poverty)
Includes bibliographical references and index.
ISBN 0-8153-1961-4 (alk. paper)
1. Afro-American single mothers—Social conditions. 2. Afro-American single mothers—Psychology. 3. Single mothers—United States—Social conditions. 4. Single mothers—United States—Psychology. 5. Single-parent family—United States. I. Title. II. Series.
HQ759.915.W57 1995
306.85'6'08996073—dc20 95-703

Printed on acid-free, 250-year-life paper
Manufactured in the United States of America

To my mother, Lena, a single mother,

for her love,
undying faith, and pride in me.

Contents

Tables

Preface

This book resulted from a study conducted as a dissertation project. The idea for the study was conceived from my work as an Educational Psychologist with children and their parents, particularly single mothers, in New York City public schools and community mental health agencies. Working predominantly with black families, in predominantly black neighborhoods in Brooklyn, Manhattan and the Bronx, New York, I had many opportunities to learn firsthand of the problems of living experienced by these families. I believed that many of the families my colleagues and I worked with experienced universal and unique problems associated with parenting, socio-economic status, and other personal issues. I also believed that many of these problems were further exacerbated by ethnicity and the stress of urban life.

Believing strongly in education, it seemed to me that parent education was an underutilized educational resource possibility for the urban black single mother parent group. I was convinced however that any attempt at developing effective parent education for this parent group required more than just the teaching of parenting skills. Among other things, parenting effectiveness can be hampered by a parent's inability to cope with the stressors of daily life, particularly if that parent had never had his or her own needs met in a variety of ways. Out of these notions came the desire to learn more about the needs of urban black single mothers. Applying Adkins Life Skills educational theory and methods provided the tool for actually accomplishing this goal.

As a graduate student, I studied and trained in the theory and use of the Life Skills educational model for program design. I later worked directly with the Life Skills model, applying its concepts, principles, and methods to teaching homeless adults job preparation skills. During these years it became clear to me that these concepts, principles, and methods could appropriately be applied to the development of a parenting program for urban black single mothers.

The challenge to conducting the study and writing the book has been attempting to transmit the urgency of the problem of ever-increasing female-headed urban black families while avoiding the reinforcement of old stereotypes. The intent of the book is the proposal of one additional, viable, educational resource that can assist urban black single mothers in need to develop themselves as parents and as persons.

The key elements of this book are the assessment of the life problems of urban black single mothers and the proposal for the design of a curriculum for a parenting/personal development program for this parent group based on assessment findings. The assessment, the findings, and the application of the Life Skills model to the development of parent education curricula is unique in the field. While the urban black single mother parent population is the subject of this study, it is not the only parent population which could benefit from this type of program. It is hoped that the reader will also recognize the growing need for comprehensively designed parent education to become an integral part of the American educational system.

Acknowledgments

Numerous people have contributed their ideas and support to the completion of this work. To all of them I am deeply grateful. Special appreciation is extended to Dr. Winthrop R. Adkins, whose vision and ideas inspired me and whose conceptual assistance throughout was indispensable. I am also indebted to Dr. Samuel Johnson whose ideas and suggestions, particularly in the conceptualization of the Single Mother Questionnaire, were invaluable. Further appreciation is extended to Dr. Margaret Jo Shepherd and Dr. Rose Marie Truglio for their helpful assistance.

I also wish to thank the many friends, colleagues and associates who helped to bring this project to fruition. Most profound thanks goes to Dr. Virginia L. Flintall, my friend and colleague, who served as a role-model, an untiring advisor, and an empathetic listener. To Dr. Nancy Boyd-Franklin, whose professional guidance was extremely helpful. To Carol Jones, who helped to collect RECON data. To Joan Rawlins, Marjorie Strong, Kathryn Lombard, Cynthia Vaughn, Doris Dennard, Marlene Ward and the late Dr. Leon McKinney, who contributed their professional and personal knowledge and insights about the psycho-social functioning of the parent group. To Donald Davis, who edited at least one draft of the manuscript and to Karen Brobst, who guided me through several computerized examinations of SMQ data.

I, most wholeheartedly, thank all of the single mothers who so enthusiastically participated in the project in the hope that it might contribute to making life better for other single mothers and their children.

Finally, my deepest gratitude goes to my family. To my husband, Herman, my daughters, Lorraine and Lisa, and my son, Darryl, who gave me love, understanding, and constant encouragement throughout. In addition, Lisa provided technical and editing support that was invaluable to the completion of this book. Without all of them, I could not have persevered.

Child, Parent, or Both?

CHAPTER I

Single Mothers: An Overview

"For the first time, more than one million babies were born to unmarried mothers in the United States in a year" (Byrd, 1991). That sentence began a news article in which it was reported that 1,005,299 babies, or 26 percent of U.S. newborns, were born to unmarried women in 1988. In the article, a spokesperson for the Center for Health Statistics notes low birth weight as a health risk for infants in this situation and points out that studies have shown that unmarried women usually get worse prenatal care, have less education and are more likely to use alcohol or drugs. More recently, statistics from the New York City Department of Health reported a dramatic increase in infant mortality rates among poor single mothers in Harlem, a predominantly black New York City community (Wasserman, 1994).

In another startling article entitled, "Juvenile Crime Study Gauges Impact of Drugs and Family," *The New York Times*, (1988), it was reported that 72 percent of over 18,000 juveniles in long-term state-operated juvenile institutions said they had not grown up with both parents. Half of those surveyed said they had lived mainly with their mothers.

An examination of overall statistics on single parenting indicates that the issue of single parent households headed by women has become a major social problem for American society today. Nationwide, in 1960, only one child in ten was reported as living in a single-parent household. By 1990 that figure had risen to more than one quarter of all American children. Eighty-nine percent of these children were reported as living with their mothers, many at or below poverty level (U.S. Bureau of the Census, 1991).

Black Single Mothers

Statistically, the issue of single mother households among blacks is more widespread. According to Byrd, the National Center for Health Statistics also reported that 63 percent of black babies born in the U.S. in 1988 were born to unmarried women. In an article entitled *Black and White in America*, (Gelman, Springen, Brailsford & Miller, 1988), concern over the rapidly growing "urban underclass" is highlighted by statistics claiming that 55 percent of families fitting this category are headed by black female single parents.

There is growing concern in the black community regarding the increase in black female-headed families due to economic, social, and educational factors. Clearly, a primary factor is economics. The reality that so many female-headed black families now live at or below the poverty level, with all the attendant problems that implies, continues to be a source of major concern. For example, one very visible result of the crisis of poverty in the 1980's was the rapidly increasing rate of homelessness among urban families headed by black women. In 1988 New York State reported that an average of 6,700 families with 13,500 children were provided with emergency housing on a daily basis. Nearly 80 percent of these families were sheltered in New York City alone and four in ten of these children were black (New York State Assembly, 1988).

What is evident is that there is a growing crisis among female-headed black families, particularly among poor families, living in urban areas. Children raised in poverty today are destined to become the disadvantaged parents of the future, proliferating the already rapid growth of the urban underclass.

Having sole responsibility for the financial, emotional and physical well-being of children, living often in dangerous communities and striving for a better life for their families presents obstacles that some mothers may have difficulty overcoming. If poor and from a disadvantaged background herself, the urban black single mother may perceive her obstacles as insurmountable and give up efforts to improve her and her family's life chances. Although all black single mothers may not need the same kind of help, readily available, appropriate resources, aimed at assisting this parent population in the areas of parenting and self-development are needed.

The rapid growth of black female-headed families within the last two decades, poses a serious threat to the economic and social opportunities available to millions of black children, placing them at risk. To allow so many black children to continue to be placed at risk at current rates through the 1990's and beyond portends a negative impact on society of staggering proportions. Clearly, this situation mandates action on many fronts.

There are a number of policy measures which need to be considered nationwide to turn things around for the future. For example, raising the minimum wage to a livable wage, prosecuting discriminatory practices in the workplace, providing better job opportunities, making affordable child care more available, increasing health services, launching a full-scale drug treatment as well as enforcement policy are some of the measures which could help. In addition, specific measures introduced into our educational system to facilitate better marital decisions, strengthen the family as a unit, help to prevent marital conflict and avoid family breakup are needed.

To address the more immediate needs of an ever-growing population of urban black single mothers and children, already caught up in the vicious cycle of poverty and despair, I propose the development of a new type of parent education program. One which recognizes the mother, not only as a parent but, as a whole person, with her own self-development needs. A parenting and personal development program of this magnitude could offer a most viable approach to helping urban black single mothers in need to acquire the information, resources and skills to solve many of the life problems they are experiencing. Therefore, an investigation of the life problems that could influence the content, scope, and nature of such a program was important to conduct.

Thus, the purpose of this study was the assessment of the psycho-social needs of urban black single mothers in order to form the basis for the design of a parenting and personal development program specifically for this parent group. Although concerned with the parenting and personal development needs of all urban black single mothers, the primary focus of the study remained with those mothers at the lower end of the socioeconomic scale.

Parent Education and Urban Black Single Mothers

Parent education, which has long been accepted as supportive of American family life, can be useful, if appropriately designed, in helping urban black single mothers, to raise emotionally and physically healthy children while helping mothers fulfill their own self-development needs. The ultimate result of developing such parent education programs would be the lowering of risk factors to a multitude of black children, now and in generations to come.

Although parent education programs in various formats have been available for some time, on a limited basis, they appear to have been less than effective in meeting the specific needs of black single mothers (Tramontana, Sherrets & Authier, 1980). One apparent difficulty seems to be that no noteworthy attempt has been made to define those specific needs and place them in an educational context. Another apparent difficulty lies perhaps in the parent education field itself where critics have been concerned with the narrow focus of most programs (Meyer, 1980), the unavailability of programs on a wide scale (Forehand, Middlebrook, Rogers & Steffe, 1983), and the fact that the development of individuals into good parents has not been given a priority status in our educational system (Weissbourd & Grimm, 1981).

While it is understood that every black single mother may not need the help of a parenting program per se, statistics and professional experience suggests that many could benefit from the parenting/self-development program model proposed by this study.

The balance of this chapter will explore the literature as it relates to the psycho-social problems of black single mothers and the effectiveness or ineffectiveness of parent education programs aimed at single parents. Lastly, a new program model for parent education, specifically designed for urban black single mothers, will be presented.

THE PROBLEMS OF BLACK SINGLE MOTHERS

The problems of black single mothers have been looked at by researchers. Although the literature is primarily concerned with the problems of poor mothers, there is evidence to suggest that it is not only poor black single mothers who might benefit from parent education programs. For example, a study conducted by the National Association of Social Workers (1987), which included poor and non-poor, minority and non-minority, and urban and rural residents, suggests that although many single mothers "view themselves as strong and resourceful", they think their lives could be improved by more and better employment and training opportunities, more affordable child care, related transportation services, and greater involvement (both financial and emotional) of fathers in their children's lives. McAdoo (1981) found that single black mothers, both middle and working class were "significantly stressed". These mothers reported their financial situations as their greatest source of stress. This source of stress was closely followed by stressors related to housing, jobs, male-female relationships, health concerns, personal habits, and legal problems. These mothers also reported that they often felt lonely and powerless, especially if they lacked social support. Hetherington, Cox & Cox (1978) report that even black single mothers who are doing well financially are struggling with other stressful problems like task overload, time pressures, and the control and discipline of their children. These findings tend to support the usefulness of looking at the needs of urban black single mothers across socioeconomic subsets.

Economics

Single parent families headed by women are most often confronted by problems resulting from economic factors; that is, unemployment, excessive numbers of unwanted children, and poverty (Gorum, 1984). Poverty is so much a part of life for American families headed by women that even many of those who work have been unable to escape its clutches. In addition, these women have received little aid from recent administrations whose policies have served to consign them and their children to poverty rolls.

The Center for the Study of Social Policy (1984), reported on three samples of working poor mothers in Georgia, Michigan, and New York City, who were negatively affected by the Omnibus Budget Reconciliation Act (OBRA) of 1981. The report on OBRA specifically explored the effects of selected federal welfare budget cuts on working poor female-headed families. The study indicated that although statistics point out that more and more single mothers entered the labor force over the past 20 years, their earnings are still considerably lower than those of single males or married couples.

In 1981, the median weekly income for families maintained by single women was $198 versus $311 for families headed by single males. Moreover, the median weekly income for married couple families with two earners was $585. The OBRA policy changes also resulted in thousands of children being cut from Aid to Families with Dependent Children (AFDC) welfare rolls and created a work disincentive by punishing mothers who chose to work. Many black single mothers were forced to give up low paying jobs if they wanted to maintain Medicaid or food stamp benefits for their families (The Center for the Study of Social Policy, 1984).

According to Gary (1983), poor black single mothers have a greater likelihood of involvement with public agencies like welfare, often due to cycles of generational dependency. Cordes (1984) hypothesizes three other factors which may also contribute to black single mothers' greater involvement with welfare agencies when compared to their white counterparts: (1) if white single mothers work, they generally tend to earn more than working black single mothers, (2) white single mothers' families are more likely to be better off financially and, (3) white single mothers' children's fathers are more likely able to afford child support.

Stigmatization and Discrimination

Families headed by single women are stressed by the stigma frequently associated with female-headed homes (Landis, 1960). Stigmatization is based on the general view of American society that both poverty and single parenthood are inferior and pathological states (Bilge & Kaufman, 1983). Discrimination, an outgrowth of stigmatization, may be experienced by single mothers in their interactions with public, private and religious organizations and agencies. Evidence of discrimination of this sort against female-headed families is well documented in the divorce literature (Grollman, 1969; Marsden, 1969).

In regard to black female-headed families, there is frequently an assumption of pathology based purely on racism. While reality indicates that many black single mothers head functional families and raise capable children, such families are still affected by stigmatization and discrimination. Evidence suggests that regardless of socioeconomic status or middle class values, black single mothers experience more difficulties in childrearing due to racial discrimination. Bagarozzi (1980) notes that although black middle-class parents may have similar goals and expectations for their children, they "find their attainment more difficult because of discrimination and prejudice which is inherent in many social, cultural and economic institutions in the United States" (p. 161).

In a society which discriminates based on race, parental/marital status, and sex, the black single mother finds herself discriminated against in at least three ways: she is female, she is black, and she is a single parent.

Divorce or Separation

The problems of divorce or separation deserve special attention in a society where both have become so common. Like their white counterparts, black couples have not been spared. Beyond the first and most startling effect of such family breakups, the sudden decline in economic standards which frequently plunges women and children into poverty, there are other major psychological negative outcomes on all members of the family. Freudenthal (1959) notes these to be: a sense of incompleteness, frustration, failure, and guilt, as well as, ambivalence between parent and child.

Burgess (1970), in reporting sociological findings regarding divorced women as compared to still married women, stated that formerly married women are more likely to feel unhappy, to lack self-confidence, to suffer from fears of being alone, and from loss of self-esteem as women. He further notes that for divorced mothers there are also the objective problems of finding the time and energy to produce income and still be the kind of mother needed to maintain discipline, educate children, and insure their positive emotional growth.

Divorce, separation, and desertion rates continue to rise within the black community, reflecting what is occurring in society generally and greatly increasing the numbers of black single mothers. According to Rodgers-Rose (1980), urban environments have contributed to the increasing numbers of black single mothers by imposing a structure that tends to separate husbands and wives. Staples (1973) suggests that while white women under thirty stand a one in three chance of having their marriages end in divorce, black women stand a one in two chance.

Belle's (1979) field study findings indicate that divorced or separated black women show higher rates of depression than divorced or separated white women. McAdoo (1981) reports that although being a single mother through divorce is usually a transitional status for white women, divorced black women tend to remain single. A significant factor contributing to this phenomenon is suggested by Wilson and Neckerman (1985) who cite a dearth of eligible black males as marriage candidates due to unemployment, incarceration, and an appalling murder rate, the leading cause of death of black males age 15 to 44. The National Urban League (1985) concludes that the ratio of black males to females has already reached a point that seriously reduces the possibility of two-parent families among blacks.

Poor Mental or Physical Health

Research studies on women's reactions to stress are useful in helping to understand behaviors which may negatively affect a single mother's parenting ability. Mental health service delivery literature indicates that women are more likely to report symptoms of psychological stress (Ilfeld, 1977; Srole, Langner, Michael, Opler & Rennie, 1961). Pearlin and Schooler's (1978) study on stress and coping showed that women from low-income groups characteristically use coping responses that exacerbate rather than reduce stress. According to Tableman, Marciniak, Johnson and Rodgers (1982), maladaptive behavior in responding to multiple stressors seems to account for the excess in symptomatology observed. Drug or alcohol abuse, child abuse or neglect, and child abandonment are types of maladaptive behaviors that can be exhibited by desperate parents experiencing multiple stressors with which they are unable to cope. Each month, in New York City alone, 450 children under the age of two enter the city's foster care system via hospitals after being deserted by their mothers (Williams, 1990).

Belle (1979) analyzed statistical data provided by the National Institute of Mental Health and concluded that there are disproportionate numbers of low income, single parent mothers of young children who are depressed. His findings suggested that high rates of depression seem to be associated with stress which derives from life conditions such as low-income, single parenthood, and responsibility for young children. As part of his 1979 study, Belle also conducted field research, to rate depression and to assess whether depression correlated with life stresses in low income black and white single mothers, resulted in a finding of a correlation between high depression scores and high stress scores. Further exploration of coping strategies suggested that the social support network was not sufficient to prevent depression. Life condition stress was composed of ongoing conditions including stress felt in employment, extended family, friends, mental health, physical health, love and marital relationships, the law, living conditions, money, education, and parenting.

Tiblier (1978) studying self-reports of stress and coping strategies of 200 adults (50 each of black men, black women, white men, and white women) found that white men and women reported their greatest concern to be their family and friends, while black men and women's greatest concern was their financial situations. Findings from this study also indicated that whites reported greater success in coping with stress than blacks.

Fisher (1984) reports that chronic fears are frequently responsible for endemic feelings of helplessness and defeat. Among poor urban black single mothers, the most serious of chronic stressful conditions frequently result from fears related to their urban environments. Such fears may include fear of homelessness due to eviction or burnout, fear of losing children because of inability to adequately provide for them, fear of hunger, and fear of crime. In addition, when faced with legal difficulties, poor urban black single mothers have little access to the protection of the legal system.

Fisher goes on to report that chronic distress can be found more frequently in situations where the safety of the neighborhood and level of housing are poor, common conditions in many urban black neighborhoods. Crowded homes, which are frequently an aspect of low income and status, are a reality for many poor black single mothers and children. These circumstances have a negative impact on both emotional and physical health. Blacks living in large urban centers are frequently victims of the communities in which they live. Regardless of socioeconomic status and upwardly mobile aspirations, housing costs and racism frequently work together to make moving out prohibitive.

A 1985 report entitled, *Statement of Community District Needs,* issued by the Department of City Planning of New York City, sets forth some of the problems encountered by blacks in predominantly black urban communities. In addition to deterioration of its housing stock, these communities face a declining economic base, high rates of unemployment, growing concentrations of low income residents, a low health index, poor sanitation and environmental conditions, and high crime rates. Increased violence in black urban communities associated with gangs and drug trafficking has many parents fearful. Recently, in one urban center, during an eight day period, "four children were killed by stray bullets as they played on the sidewalks, toddled in their grandmothers' kitchens or slept soundly in their own beds." In the ensuing months, six more children were wounded by gunfire in the same city (Cronin, Pomper & Simpson, 1990). Fears for the safety of children in such crime-ridden communities are often a major deterrent to mothers seeking employment, since a job would take them away from the home for many hours without adequate supervision of children. These environmental factors contribute significantly to the decline in mental and physical health of urban black single mothers.

Declining Support Systems and Isolation

Traditionally, black single parents have tended to utilize informal rather than formal support networks and helping resources (Gorum, 1983). Hendricks, Howard and Gary (1981) investigating where urban blacks would most likely go for help with a serious problem found that the second most frequently consulted source of help was informal such as family, friends, and clergy, while the first was an institutional setting such as a hospital. Least frequently consulted was a doctor or psychiatrist. Hill's (1972) findings on single parents suggested that the kinship bond was most commonly practiced for the psycho-social welfare of the single parent and that this bond appeared to be stronger among black families.

More recently, some researchers have become fearful that the strong tradition of extended families among blacks may be "breaking down." Height (1985) speculates that black families are undergoing a forced metamorphosis, particularly in urban areas, in regard to extended family households. The overall results are smaller, poorer family units, with many young mothers living in isolation. Boyd-Franklin (1989), in discussing differences between functional and dysfunctional black single-parent families notes, among the characteristics of functional families, the possession and utilization of support systems.

Ladner's research (cited in Cordes, 1984) concluded that without adequate intervention, a single mother's daughter is likely to repeat the pattern of early birth. Ladner notes, increasingly when this occurs, young grandmothers, who are often still responsible for small children of their own and working, are less willing or able to extend the kinds of supports, such as baby-sitting, which were previously available.

Cordes notes, "Some researchers and family advocates believe extended kin networks among blacks have been weakened by greater geographic mobility (e.g., rural to urban relocation), the hard times many black families have experienced in recent years, and simultaneous cuts in public social services." In its report of single black mothers in Georgia, Michigan, and New York City, The Center for the Study of Social Policy (1984) indicated that the majority of the children of single black mothers lived with their mothers alone. The ratio of mother and children only households to those where other adults were also present was 83:17 in New York City, 69:31 in Michigan, and 52:48 in Georgia. In general, the "other adults" in Georgia were the mother's siblings or parents. The report speculates that differences in the housing market, less mobility, and degree of poverty tend to account for the significant differences in mother-children versus mother-children-extended family homes in Georgia and New York.

Finally, in urban environments many poor black families headed by women have become isolated by the exodus of well-off blacks moving to better neighborhoods (Gelman et al., 1988):

> The isolation of the underclass was a hazard of the civil rights movement. As it succeeded, more educated and entrepreneurial blacks moved to integrated neighborhoods, taking their gifts with them. It is an irony that distresses middle-class blacks: a deep class divide among blacks themselves (p. 20).

In summary, the research findings cited above suggest that black single mothers face a variety of problems. These problems include poverty, discrimination, lack of available marriage partners, stress caused mental and physical health problems, and declining support systems. In addition, some black single mothers experience feelings of guilt, frustration, loneliness, depression, anger, fear, and helplessness.

Greatest concern is expressed for the poor black single mother because of the greater number of factors placing her and her children at risk but, there is recognition that middle class black single mothers are possibly also under significant stress. Although there was no mention in the literature regarding the impact these varying problems and psycho-social difficulties have on parenting ability, it is known that stress greatly influences behavior (Stack, 1974).

Researchers who have studied the strengths of black females have noted a chief characteristic to be the black woman's realistic approach to her own resources, the ability to use existing resources and a determination to survive (Ladner, 1971). The rising tide, over the last two decades, of urban black female-headed families in crisis may indicate that there are fewer and fewer of those existing resources to call upon, especially in the cities. Furthermore, if researchers are correct in their findings of declining kin networks and other types of supports, then it would explain why so many families appear to be losing ground.

In order to resolve some of these problems, black female-headed families need the support of their communities to help them economically, socially, and psychologically. "Many one-parent families are realizing that they are capable of raising healthy children with the assistance of supportive networks within their family, religious institutions, and the community" (McAdoo, 1981). Hill (1968) has long claimed that it is society's challenge to develop institutions, value systems, supports, and programs that will enable the single parent family to function effectively.

PARENT EDUCATION PROGRAMS

Historically, some form of parent education has existed in the U.S. since the early 1800's. Literature advising parents dates back almost as far as the printing press (Authier, Sherrets, & Tramontana, 1980). Parent education groups have been recorded as far back as 1815 (Bridgeman, 1930; Sunley, 1955; Croake & Glover, 1977).

Arguments for the continued need for parent education are numerous. Clark-Stewart (1978) suggests its need because of the limited experience individuals will have due to smaller family size, increased child care outside the home, and isolation from other family members during child-rearing years. Bigner (1979) argues that the modeling learned from adults' own parents is inadequate to deal with the problems of contemporary parenthood. Bronfenbrenner (1972) and LeMasters (1977) argue its importance due to the changes in family structure, such as, an increased number of working mothers and single parents.

Parent education has become a major topic in the divorce literature in recognition of the significant demands for time, energy, and money placed on custodial parents, whether mothers or fathers (Hale, 1983).

In an article providing a framework for examining parent education programs, Authier, et al., (1980) reports on the various categories of parents with special needs who can be served through parent education including teenage parents, foster and adoptive parents, parents of children with handicaps, abusive and neglectful parents, and single parents.

Along with the recognition of a continued need for parent education has come the realization that change is also needed (Stephans, 1982).

Parent education programs have been effectively addressed toward an array of problem behaviors and issues of children; tantrums (Williams, 1959); enuresis and encopresis (Madsen, 1965); retardation and brain damage (Patterson, Jones, Whittier, & Wright, 1965); and typical child management problems (Hall, Axelrod, Tyler, Grief, Jones, & Robertson, 1972; O'Dell, 1974).

Targeted Parent Populations

Typically, parent education has been designed for specific parent populations. Among social support programs for new parents, a number have targeted low-income adolescent mothers and have reported varying results (Wandersman, 1981). Badger (1981) and Porter (1979) report on group support programs that have among their goals the development of parent skills. Similar programs have been designed for middle income couples (Dickie & Gerber, 1980; Wandersman, 1978). Wandersman found that parents who participate in groups for new parents generally attend consistently, enjoy participation, learn some relevant information, and feel less alone.

Most typical among parent education offerings are a number of group approaches aimed toward improving child-rearing methods. Lamb and Lamb (1978) define these approaches as the formal attempt to increase parents' awareness and facility of the skills of parenting. Among the most popular of these are various behavioral approaches, for example, Parent Effectiveness Training (PET), and Adlerian approaches. Although, in theory, these formats are not aimed at any specific parent group, they tend to be most popular with middle-class parents (Dembo, Sweitzer, & Lauritzen, 1985).

Interestingly, there have not been many programs claiming to have been designed specifically for single parents and this researcher could not find one that was designed specifically for black single mothers. The following examples are representative, in terms of design, of the extremely limited number of programs that have attempted to primarily serve single parent populations. For the most part, these programs can be characterized as virtuoso, one-time efforts that were defunded almost as quickly as begun, whether or not they appeared to be successful. A result of this kind of limited, quick-fix, one-shot approach to parent education program design for single parents has been that no one program has lasted long enough to make a discernible impact on the population nor, provide the cumulative knowledge needed to positively effect the field.

Programs for Single Parents

The Operation Cope Family Centers (COPE). COPE was designed for disadvantaged young mothers during the 1970's (National Council of Negro Women, 1975). COPE was funded by the U.S. Department of Health, Education, and Welfare for one year. The project was experimental in nature, with stated aims to involve participants in an adult basic education process that would provide them with a better ability to "communicate and computate"; to help parents to acquire elementary "coping mechanisms" that would increasingly enable them to handle the pressures of educational deprivation; to involve participants in training that would prepare them to be more effective parents and citizens; to offer paraprofessional staff members adequate opportunities to establish a foundation for future career growth and upward mobility; to involve parents in learning experiences that would broaden and enrich the scope of their family life; to provide participants with the added support of a network of volunteers who would bolster the center's operation and, to establish opportunities for the participants to acquire needed services through the project's linkages with other community agencies and organizations.

Components of the program curriculum were developed based on the expressed educational and vocational interests and needs of the learners and focused on teaching skills subjects such as typing, sewing, and arts and crafts. Participants expected to be taught these skills in ways which would equip them to be employed at some future date. Job placement was not a part of the program. Other components of the curriculum involved teaching basic reading and math skills and teaching child development.

According to the National Council of Negro Women, COPE was reported to be a "dynamic, joyous, and fulfilling" educational experience for participants and staff alike, however, the program lost its funding in 1974 and was discontinued.

According to its developers, Operation COPE was an attempt to help disadvantaged young mothers educationally and vocationally and to teach and promote parenting and citizenship skills along the way. Some components of the curriculum were based on expressed interests of participants and, participants received help in entitlement areas as well as in support networking. Seemingly, embodied in the program concept, was opportunity for participants to enhance self-esteem and self-confidence by successfully completing one or more of the academic or vocational skills courses. However, there was no provision in the design for evaluating enhanced self-esteem or confidence and there was no mention of how mothers who were unsuccessful in completing academic or vocational courses were handled. Other needs of participants were apparently not assessed and, therefore, not provided for in the curriculum.

Parenting Alone Successfully (PALS). PALS, designed by Leavitt and Davis (1980) was aimed at a target population of single parent families with children who were experiencing behavior problems. The primary focus of the program was teaching parents behavior management skills. Parents were subsequently trained in behavior management techniques for controlling their children's problem behaviors. A needs assessment approach was used initially to assess parental needs in terms of child management. At the time of the authors' report, the program was apparently still in existence but not widely available.

PALS is an example of a completely child-centered parent education program with primary emphasis on children's behavior problems and a needs assessment focused strictly on child-management needs. Although aimed at single parents, PALS makes no attempt to relate to possible parental psycho-social issues that may be impacting, or contributing to, the behavior problems of children.

The Single Parent Resource Center. According to a project report by the Child care Switchboard Single Parent Resource Center (1977), on their own program, the aim of their project was to "provide a viable model for provision of social services to single parents." Specific goals of the project were stated as follows: to provide information, through the child care switchboard, in the areas of child care, housing referrals, and welfare counseling and to refer callers to the single parent unit when appropriate for peer counseling and information; to provide a drop-in support group for single parents to meet and share support for a single parent lifestyle and to promote the formation of peer support networks; to provide workshops on single parent topics of interest; to provide peer counseling; and, to extend outreach and technical assistance through the utilization of media. Following a one year experiment, the project lost its funding.

The Single Parent Resource Center appeared to be a loosely structured entitlement and network referral resource rather than a program. Although stated goals were laudable, the center seemed to operate on a crisis or as-needed services model, with no curriculum development.

Summary of Parent Programs for Single Parents

In summary, Operation COPE, PALS, and The Single Parent Resource Center, are all examples of types of parent education programs intended for single parents, which attempted to embody some of the needed concepts and services.

Although most of the stated aims and goals of each program seemed appropriate, specific plans for obtaining these goals were either lacking or vague in operational descriptions. There appeared to be a lack of structure in all and a definite need for an assessment of target groups beyond vocational and educational interests or child-management techniques. Finally, it is equally important if a program is to be available to its targeted population, that it be replicable. None of the programs reviewed appeared to have that capability and, according to Clark-Stewart (1978), the unavailability of parent education programs generally is a major criticism of the field.

Program Effectiveness

Despite the reported wide array of problems and parent groups that programs have been directed toward, there has been little evidence to support claims of effectiveness. Overall, reviewers who have looked at the reported "successes" by authors of parent education programs generally, have had difficulty identifying actual effectiveness with parents and children (O'Dell, 1974). Programs that have demonstrated success have primarily focused on changing specific problem behaviors of children, for example, problems of school phobia (Patterson, 1965).

The need for a dual-leveled approach. Tramontana et al. (1980) notes factors contributing to program ineffectiveness to be irrelevance of curriculum content; failure to note cultural, racial, and socioeconomic differences among parents; failure to facilitate differing parental goals and failure to note parental perceptions of themselves as parents and as persons. Meyer (1980) contends that "parents who have not had support to maximize their own growth are not prepared to adequately enhance the growth of their children" (p.8). Like Meyer, Stephans (1982) advocates a "dual-leveled" approach to parent education, (e.g., one which recognizes that development of the parent is as important as that of the child).

The importance of a dual-leveled approach to curriculum development and delivery in parent education can perhaps be summarized in the following statement by Stephans describing "good parenting":

> Regardless of the information and understanding parents have of the emotional needs of the child, it may be that their own emotional capability of meeting these needs is the primary determinant of "good parenting" (p. 17).

The value of needs assessment. The value of needs assessment in program design has been well documented in the literature (Datta, 1978; Heinkel, 1974; Sarthory, 1977). Brackhaus (1984) has found needs assessment to be both cost-effective and essential for adult education programs, noting that "accountability is increased because needs assessments provide a rational basis for decisions and increase the likelihood that programs will be successful" (p. 237).

In summary, although parent education program effectiveness is dependent on many factors, two of the most important appear to be needs assessment, in the initial stage of program design, and a dual-leveled approach in the development of curricula. A new model for parent education program design is needed which incorporates these essential elements.

A NEW PROGRAM MODEL FOR PARENT EDUCATION

Given the above, an important question to be asked is, how can an effective parent education program for urban black single mothers be constructed and what are the essential elements to be included in such a program? Based on the literature review, it seems clear that any program should have two tiers: one that focuses on what parents need to learn to be more effective parents to their children and one that focuses on what they need to learn as individuals to improve the quality of their own lives as adults.

It is also clear from the literature that the content of the curricula for such programs must be relevant to the parents and take into consideration their concerns and the problems that they are experiencing as a result of their marital and socioeconomic status, their race, and their urban environment. Also, for such programs to be effective, they must help the parents clarify and achieve their own goals, solve problems important to them, and enhance their competence and perception of themselves as parents and persons. Finally, such programs, if they are to have impact, must embody a structure and process of learning that produces lasting behavioral change and should be capable of wide replicability.

Need for a Curriculum Development Model

The construction of an effective parenting and personal development program which can encompass in its design, all of the essential elements identified above, requires a curriculum model and curriculum development process that is, above all, sensitive to the special learning needs of a given target population. A review of different curriculum models (Adkins, 1973, 1984; Grundy, 1987; Joyce, 1971; Pinar, 1981; Tyler, 1971) revealed few models specifically developed for the problems and learning styles of disadvantaged adults. Also, most were developed for subject areas such as science, literature, the arts, or to enhance literacy, etc., (Unruh & Unruh, 1984).

One curriculum model was identified which had been developed specifically for disadvantaged adults and which was aimed at "helping a particular target group learn to cope with the predictable psycho-social problems of life they experience as workers, persons, parents, marital partners, and citizens." Operating from the perspective of a counseling psychologist, Adkins (1984) developed a complete curriculum development system which included:

1) a systematic process of psycho-social needs assessment for deriving the content from the actual life problems of the target group,

2) a Four Stage Structured Inquiry Learning Model for curriculum development and program delivery aimed at facilitating affective, cognitive, and behavioral learning with a problem-solving framework,

3) a set of curriculum design principles for helping learners identify their own values, strengths, and goals and for dignifying their existing knowledge, skills, and experiences,

4) methods for using video, computers, and group dynamics technologies to facilitate learning and the replicability of the program in multiple settings,

5) a successful career development program, based on this method, now widely in use for this population,

6) a companion, field tested, Life Skills Educator Staff Development Program to help teachers, counselors, and administrators deliver the program effectively. This is also widely in use for staff working with this population,

7) a dissemination process for helping to ensure widespread use of developed programs.

These characteristics of Adkins' approach to program development appeared to fit most closely with what the literature on parent education programs indicated was needed to develop more effective parent education programs. Particularly attractive is its needs assessment process which is an integral part of program development, and its potential for use in developing programs from a dual-leveled parent/person perspective, focused on psycho-social skill learning needs. The final portion of this chapter reviews the work of the Adkins Life Coping Skills Model (hereafter referred to as "Life Skills") and relates its structure and design elements to parent education for the urban black single mother parent population.

LIFE SKILLS EDUCATION

Life Skills Education is defined as "essentially a program area and an innovative method for teaching and learning" (Adkins, 1970, p. 112). It can perhaps be best understood, as described by Adkins (1984) as "an effort to create a more effective delivery system for making counseling/learning sources available on a mass scale to large numbers of people from different target groups who are not now receiving help" (p. 44). "Life Skills programs are rooted in developmental and psycho educational theory and focus on the predictable life tasks and problems of diverse populations" (Cullinane, 1984, p. 15). Originally, "Life Skills" served as a descriptor of the kind of psychological and social competencies usually identified as needed by counselors and therapists (Adkins, Rosenberg, & Sharar, 1965). The term "Life Skills" however is now associated with a wide variety of trivial and profound cognitive and motoric as well as psychological problems (Adkins, 1984). "Life Skills" is used herein as originally employed by Adkins.

Life Skills Theory and Rationale

The Life Skills model was proposed by Adkins (1974) as a "fifth curriculum," intended to focus on "biological, psychological, social, moral, vocational, marital, and other aspects of personal development pertinent to the needs of individuals from different target groups (age, sex, ethnic group, socioeconomic status, educational level, state of health, etc.). The curriculum consequently would be based on a specific analysis of the tasks of normal development as identified by research and through an examination of the life problems of different groups. The curriculum would be directed toward providing the essential knowledge, understanding, and skill for making and implementing decisions important for effective personal development. It would be a competency based program designed to foster the behavioral mastery and attitudinal change necessary for dealing with the predictable situations of modern life" (p. 512).

Life Skills is based on several assumptions, a central one being that large numbers of people face common life situations thus, they are trying to solve similar psychological and social problems (Adkins, 1984). Contained within this central assumption is the notion of the individual as expert on his or her problems. Adkins emphasized this notion, saying that the members of the target group themselves are the first experts on their problems; that is, members of the target group are most often the ones who can best identify "where they hurt." Secondly, that there is another kind of expert on the problem, those who have extensive experience with members of the target group, (e.g., "significant others" who have had opportunity to observe those problems from a distance) and who know something about solutions to those problems.

Among the other basic assumptions of Life Skills is the assumption that if a problem is experienced by a number of people in similar ways, a common learning program can be developed that will reflect not only the particular structure of the problem but also the special experiences and learning styles of the target group. Another assumption is that although there are a limited number of workable solutions to given problems, representing different combinations of different solution elements, several of these solutions can be "understood, defined, parsed, and made available to people to select from." Finally, a last assumption is that a learner's individuality can be "protected and enhanced by a program model that encourages each one to take responsibility for his or her own learning through a process of inquiry that helps learners make their own value choices and create their own syntheses at their own pace" (Adkins, 1984, p. 52). These assumptions make it reasonable to consider the creation of common programs to solve the common problems of specific target groups.

Limitations of Traditional Counseling

The limitations of traditional counseling have been well documented in the literature as they relate to personal, vocational, and career development (Cullinane, 1985; Lovett, 1984; Manuele, 1980). Inherent in all of the assumptions of Life Skills, is the notion of Life Skills as a counseling/learning process. Adkins (1974) advocates the Life Skills approach for the disadvantaged learner as opposed to traditional counseling methods based primarily on insight and awareness models. Noting the increasing importance of traditional counseling in the learning environment for facilitating coping skill development, Adkins observed the following limitations of counseling as typically conducted:

> 1. The wide range of problems and issues discussed prevents adequate treatment of any one, and rapidly overextends the counselor's competence.
> 2. The focus tends to be on communications problems and human relationships and thereby ignores many problems students have in coping with other aspects of reality.
> 3. Without structure, students find it difficult to sustain focused discussion, and instead tend to flit from problem to problem with insufficient attention or effort on any one topic.
> 4. Longer range coping problems dealing with educational and career and development tend to be pushed aside in favor of more compelling concerns.
> 5. The goal tends to be increased insight on the assumption that this will lead indirectly to changed behavior; yet students get little help in translating insight into action in any sustained way.
> 6. The emphasis on group process tends to obscure the need for goal-directed behavior.
> 7. The lack of adequate means for acquiring new knowledge and testing old assumptions tends to encourage a sharing and perpetuation of misconceptions and ignorance.

> 8. An emphasis on verbal exchange with a means for relating talk to action and practicing new behaviors tends to lead students to become enamored with discussion for its own sake (p. 510).

In addition to the limitations described above, Adkins noted the unavailability of trained counselors, and the frequent problem of poorly trained counselors, particularly those working with disadvantaged populations.

The Four Stage Learning Model

Life Skills Education provides a Four Stage Structured Inquiry Learning Model which allows flexibility and adaptability and makes it a suitable adult education learning system for a variety of adult learners and learning areas. Learning units are implemented in a small group setting of members of the target population. Adkins (1974) describes the model as follows:

> The four-stage model is a sequence of learning experiences which are designed to frame the problem in an exciting, motivationally arousing way, dignify what the student already knows about the problem-task, add what he needs to know for mastery of the task and give him experience in translating his knowledge into action (p. .518).

The Stimulus Stage. Each Life Skills learning unit begins with an emotionally arousing video vignette which frames a specific problem. The main objectives of this stage are the framing of the problem, the emotional stimulation of the students, the focusing of their attention on the problem, and the creation of readiness for discussion and the sharing of ideas.

The Evocation Stage. The Evocation Stage provides opportunity for a structured discussion. The Life Skills Educator (LSE) leads the discussion through a series of questions. The Evocation serves a number of purposes, namely, making the student aware of how much he and others know about the problem (dignifying the learner), facilitating definition of the problem, encouraging the free expression of ideas and feelings on a focused topic in a supportive, non-judgmental atmosphere, and familiarizing students with multiple sources of knowledge. During this stage, students' comments are recorded by the LSE on a flipchart or blackboard, in their own words. The process of evocation allows the learners to help in identifying learning objectives which have meaning for them.

The Objective Inquiry Stage. In the Objective Inquiry, group members begin to explore a variety of other sources of knowledge about the problems they are experiencing. A number of prepared learning resources are made available and group members are encouraged to select from them according to their preferred learning style. Through exploration of such resources as books, audiotapes, videotapes, and feedback from experts in various fields, group members not only obtain useful information about specific problem areas but also learn the skills of inquiry and resource identification.

The Application Stage. During the Application Stage, group members have an opportunity to translate their new knowledge into actual behaviors. New behaviors are practiced in and out of the classroom. In the classroom, new behaviors are videotaped and feedback is given by the group and the LSE to the learner.

Life Skills Program Development

Life Skills units, once developed, are intended to be used and reused indefinitely. Units are thus cost effective with long term usage.

The development of Life Skills units involves the following:

Needs assessment. Life Skills methodology initially requires a comprehensive needs assessment, designed to survey the overall coping problems of a specific group. After problems are selected for development, a more in-depth needs assessment is carried out with additional members of the same group.

Derivation of competencies. Problems derived from in-depth needs assessment are then stated in terms of the behaviors needed to solve them and eventually become learning objectives for learning units.

Program design. A plan for the development of a four-stage learning unit, which makes use of Adkins' Structured Inquiry Learning Model, is then constructed. This plan specifies all of the learning activities, the media used, and the sequence.

Development of materials. Life Skills units usually include video, print, and audio materials.

Testing and evaluation. A fully developed Life Skills unit is first tested out in a protected setting by an LSE (who is a combination counselor and teacher). Life Skills staff are carefully selected according to specified criteria and are trained in small, experiential groups to make effective use of the group process and the Four Stage Learning Model. An evaluation focusing on intrinsic aspects of the unit provides data for revisions. Following revisions, the unit is then tested again in a field setting, evaluated, and revised. After this revision, the unit is ready for publication.

Installation. Published learning units are usually installed into existing educational settings such as colleges, churches, community agencies, and learning centers for particular target groups. It is important to orient administrators and supervisors to the new program so that they fully understand it and its requirements. Sessions of actual use of the units with administrators provides them with the necessary criteria for selecting LSE's. LSE's are trained in Life Skills theory and concepts as well as in how to carry out the teaching and counseling so important to the Life Skills program.

Life Skills Program Delivery

It is important to say, that in delivery of fully developed Life Skills learning units, where a participant begins, in terms of content of the program, is an administrative decision usually based on initial assessment of each participant at program entry. Typically, a suggestion of sequence of learning units is part of the design of the program, (e.g., unit one typically precedes unit two, etc.). No matter where a learner starts, however, the process of the four-stage model, and the way in which learning resources are developed, provides the learner with the essential psychological transition necessary to accomplish behavior change.

Sequence of delivery of the four-stage learning process. The four-stage learning process has a sequence of delivery designed to help the learner in the following ways:

- the learner becomes a member of the group, eliminating a sense of isolation,

- the learner experiences having her ideas listened to and even recorded on a flipchart,
- the learner is made to feel that her feelings, experiences, and thoughts are listened to in a way that makes her feel dignified,
- the learner is led, step-by-step through exercise after exercise that provide knowledge in interesting ways and,
- the learner is helped to translate this knowledge into new behaviors that are empowering.

This sequence of delivery of the four-stage learning process is repeated again and again, regardless of the particular content of a learning unit.

IMPLICATIONS OF THE LIFE SKILLS MODEL FOR PARENT EDUCATION

The Life Skills model can be viewed as meeting parent education needs because it can be used for helping adults learn coping strategies for the difficult life problems they experience. In addition, the model incorporates important pedagogical concepts for adult education; that is, learning should be problem-centered, learning should be experience-centered, experience should be meaningful to the learner, the learner must be free to look at the experience, the goals must be set and the search organized by the learner, and the learner must have feedback about progress toward goals (Adkins, 1970). Adkins' experiences with disadvantaged adult learners indicated that they needed additional supports in terms of problem identification, structured and focused discussion, goal setting and reflection, and opportunity to practice newly learned skills and behaviors if their learning experience was to be meaningful and successful.

Specifically, and first, in terms of parent education program development, the Life Skills model provides for an analysis of tasks of normal development of the target group through research and an examination of problems in living. Second, resulting curricula are directed toward providing knowledge, understanding, and skill for making and implementing decisions important for effective personal development. Third, and finally, use of the model as conceived has the potential of making parent education available to large numbers of parents who have never received help. The replicability, on a mass scale, of parent education programs based on the Life Skills model will be discussed later in the study.

Adkins (1984) has defined Life Skills as "an effort to improve the rigor of the learning inherent in the counseling process" (p. 44). He outlined three major assumptions of counseling which are the basis of the Life Skills model:

> 1. Counseling is a process designed to help people cope more effectively with the predictable developmental problems, crises, and problems in living they confront at various stages of their lives. Such problems are those that cause emotional distress, which if resolved effectively, can lead to satisfaction and the effective use of one's talents but which, if not resolved, can lead to patterns of anger, alienation, and despair.
>
> 2. Counseling is primarily a process for facilitating personal growth and, therefore, it should be available on a preventive, not just a remedial, basis for all people who need help at the various stages of their development.
>
> 3. Counseling is fundamentally a learning process in which the person with the problem is helped to acquire new knowledge, attitudes, and behavior which will permit him or her to take action to resolve the problem (p. 51).

These assumptions apply directly to the underlying concerns of this study:

1. The urban black single mother faces the "predictable" developmental tasks of parenting at the same time she faces daily crisis and problems in living, often with little or no help. If the emotional distress caused by these problems is not resolved they may have a major impact on her ability to parent effectively as well as on her ability to develop herself fully;

2. the introduction of pedagogically sound principles along with counseling in a parent education program for urban black single mothers could greatly enhance opportunities for "personal growth" and development, and,

3. helping overburdened urban black single mothers acquire new knowledge, attitudes, and behavior, which will improve their and their

children's lives, justifies applying the model to parent education programs designed for this group.

SUMMARY

The American confidence in the strength of the "traditional" family has been shaken by the rapid increase of single parent households. In particular, single parent households headed by women have become a major social concern across the nation. Among blacks, female-headed households have increased at a disproportionately high rate, especially in the cities. Growing concern is primarily linked with the overwhelming evidence of poverty in female-headed households and, resultingly, the staggering numbers of children growing up "at risk" in these poverty-stricken environments.

The unprecedented increase over the last two decades in black female-headed families appears to be related to many factors, including high rates of pregnancy among black teenagers, declining numbers of black males available for marriage, and other sociological factors, such as discrimination, disadvantaged backgrounds, limited education levels, lack of job skills, and migrations to depressed urban environments.

The literature suggests that there are a number of stressors and psycho-social difficulties experienced by urban black single mothers that need to be addressed. The impact of these negative factors raises concerns about the ability of some, particularly among the underclass, urban black single mothers, to parent adequately and effectively without assistance. In addition, there is evidence in the literature to suggest that some middle class urban black single mothers may also be in need of help.

Parent education is a concept historically viewed as supportive of families. Yet, the research indicates that virtually no resources have been directed toward developing supportive programs of this nature for the black single mother parent population. The few examples found have generally been limited in scope, availability, and quality.

One approach to resolving some of the problems experienced by urban black single mothers is through the introduction of well designed parent education programs developed specifically for this parent group. Curricula for these programs would be developed from comprehensive assessments of the actual problems and needs of the target population. Since there is no indication that this type of comprehensive psycho-social needs assessment (e.g., assessment of parenting and other life problems as well as feelings and attitudes) has ever been conducted with this parent group, this study will break new ground in the parent education field with its novel and exploratory approach.

The Life Skills Education Program Model offers the most appropriate methodology for this study in that it; (1) provides a process for assessing the life problems of new target populations, (2) places those life problems into an educational context for curricula design, and (3) maps a strategy for mass availability and program development.

QUESTIONS TO BE ANSWERED

This study was conducted to assess the psycho-social needs of urban black single mothers, as perceived by them, and to delineate those needs for use in the design of a parenting and personal development program based on the Adkins Life Coping Skills Program Model.

Answers to the following questions were sought:

1. What are the psycho-social problems experienced by urban black single mothers as parents and as persons?

2. How would experienced black clinicians interpret the problems and what kind of knowledge and skills do they think are appropriate to help in solving them?

3. To what extent are the psycho-social problems of the study group shared by a larger group of urban black single mothers, or in other words, how normative are the problems for the target group?

4. How do urban black single mothers use helping resources?

5. What learning tracks and what learning objectives for a parenting and personal development program for urban black single mothers can be derived from the psycho-social problems of the study group?

CHAPTER II

An Assessment of the Needs of Urban Black Single Mothers

PROCEDURES

This chapter defines and describes the procedures used to assess the psycho-social problems of urban black single mothers and to establish the pervasiveness of these problems in this population. The procedures described are (1) Reconnaissance Interviews (group needs assessments of representative samples of the target population), (2) Clinician Interviews (individual interviews with mental health professionals having extensive experience with members of the target population), and (3) the Single Mother Questionnaire (a questionnaire developed from Reconnaissance and Clinical Interview findings as a means for assessing additional members of the target population).

PHASES

The Derivative Phase

As will be described in detail below, Reconnaissance Interviews were conducted to identify the psycho-social problems perceived by urban black single mothers as significant. This phase of the study can be described as the Derivative Phase since the purpose was to derive from the population itself a preliminary taxonomy of problems.

The Interpretive Phase

Clinician Interviews provided other perspectives by experienced observers of this population. The purpose of the Clinician Interviews was to aid the researcher in interpreting the problem data derived from the population itself. Thus, this can be described as the Interpretive Phase of the study.

The Normative Phase

Through a process of analysis of the Reconnaissance and Clinician Interview data the Single Mother Questionnaire (SMQ) was devised. The SMQ was designed in three parts. Part I (Personal and Socioeconomic Characteristics) was designed to assess characteristics of the sample. Part II (Use of Helping Resources) examined the sample's use of helping resources. Part III (Problem Statements) consisted of problem statements derived from psycho-social problems identified in Reconnaissance Interviews and which were interpreted through the perspectives of the clinicians and the heightened understanding of the researcher. The purpose for developing the SMQ was to provide a means for determining the pervasiveness of problems among a larger sample of black single mothers. Frequency of occurrence was needed to establish pervasiveness. This phase of data collection can best be described as the Normative Phase.

The Instructional Objectives Design Phase

During this phase, Reconnaissance Interview data were analyzed through a clustering and categorizing process designed to narrow down problem areas and produce a set of learning tracks. In the creation of Life Skills programs, refined learning tracks facilitate the selection and eventual development of Life Skills learning units. This culminating phase of educational design is best described as the Instructional Objectives Design Phase.

THE UNIQUE ROLE OF THE RESEARCHER

It is important to remember that the ultimate aim of the variety of techniques used to collect data for this study was to understand the psycho-social problems of the target group in its own terms. This educational process is enhanced by conferring with significant others who have observed the target group and its problems firsthand. The story unfolds over time, as one set of interviews helps the researcher to know better how to probe in subsequent interviews. The researcher becomes increasingly better educated about the nature, subtleties and interplay of problems, thus, the researcher is by design, an intrinsic part of the process and a major instrument of the research.

CHRONOLOGY OF STUDY PHASES AND PROCEDURES

As previously described, the study design consisted of four parts: the Derivative, Interpretive, Normative and Instructional Objectives Design Phases. Also, as previously described, the design of the study required that procedures utilized in some of the phases be conducted concurrently rather than sequentially (e.g., Reconnaissance Interviews and Clinician Interviews, etc.). This overlapping of procedures and phases is justified since the initiation of one phase of the study is frequently dependent on data gathered during another phase. For example, during the Derivative phase, each Reconnaissance Interview was affected by previous ones in that questions derived from the analysis of earlier Reconnaissance data enhanced subsequent data collection. In addition, phases of the study were affected by other phases as when Clinician Interviews in the Interpretive phase affected the analysis of data derived from Reconnaissance Interviews in the Derivative phase and, the results of both the Derivative and Interpretive Phases formulated the basis for the Instructional Objectives Design Phase. Finally, procedures in both the Derivative and Interpretive phases profoundly affected the development of the Single Mother Questionnaire in the Normative phase of the study.

Each of the data collection phases and procedures are described in great detail below. The chronological overlapping of procedures and phases and the effect each had on the other, in terms of data interpretation, will be further clarified.

THE DERIVATIVE PHASE

Reconnaissance Interviews

Description of Process. The "Reconnaissance Interview" (hereafter: RECON) is a group interview process developed by Adkins (1974) as a method for psycho-social needs assessment. The RECON consists of a series of in-depth, structured group interviews in which the researcher, using a number of counseling and research techniques, elicits from the target population statements of psycho-social problems. From a series of interviews with different groups of the same population, recurrent problem statements about a range of life concerns emerge. These recurrent problem statements are subsequently categorized, sorted, combined and compared with those from relevant scholarly literature. Problem statements are also derived from interviews with "significant others" (in this case, mental health clinicians) who have had the opportunity to observe these problems firsthand. Adkins describes how the RECON is utilized as a method of needs assessment:

> Using a method that I have termed "Reconnaissance", the design team tries to find out from a target population "where they hurt". The aim is to find what psychological and social problems the individuals cannot solve, the problems in living they face that cause them emotional pain and distress, such as fear, anxiety, despair, boredom, or hate. The assumption is that beneath the surface of the emotion lies a problem that cannot be solved. Through extensive group and individual interviews the design team makes a major effort to understand the problems as perceived by the person having them (p. 49).

RECON Procedures. For this study, RECON interviews were conducted as follows: The RECON interviewer arranged to meet with a small group of members of the target population (five to eight persons). Every effort was made to select the most comfortable setting possible since, ideally, a RECON session should run for approximately three hours. After explaining the purpose of the meeting, assuring anonymity in presenting the results and establishing group rapport, the interviewer began to solicit the needs and concerns of group members.

Using a variety of counseling and group work techniques, which included: reflecting feelings, paraphrasing statements, asking divergent and convergent questions, summarizing, eliciting comparisons and greater specificity, checking responses and obtaining feedback, the interviewer attempted to help individuals in the group to identify and state problems which they were experiencing. The interviewer reinforced comments, being careful to avoid judgmental behaviors or statements.

Special attention was paid to problems reflecting the emotional responses of fear, anger, despair, and alienation. At the same time, statements indicating joy, pleasure, and satisfaction were also recognized, encouraged and reinforced. Once the problems were identified, individuals were encouraged to describe the personal consequences of these problems, to discuss what they perceived to be the causes of the problems and, finally, to relate their attempts to solve the problems.

In the group setting, participants were encouraged to express their concurrence or disagreement with individual statements, explain how problems were experienced by them and offer additional problems during the discussion. Throughout the group discussion, the interviewer probed for specific details and examples in order to obtain fuller descriptions of the problems from the group.

Discussion progressed from broad, non-threatening problem statements at the beginning of the RECON to more specific and personally sensitive problem statements toward the end.

During the interview, the interviewer, or an assistant, recorded each problem statement (or its essence) on an index card. Care was taken to record the statement in the person's own words. Each recorded statement was then displayed on the walls of the room. Displaying the statements assured contributing group members that they had been heard and provided them opportunities to correct, modify, or elaborate on their statements. The recorded and displayed problem statements became permanent records of the RECON interview for later use by the researcher.

Displayed problem statements were arranged and rearranged in logical clusters as the interview continued. When the number of new problem statements offered began to diminish, the interviewer slowly brought the discussion to a close and thanked group members for their participation.

RECON interviews were repeated with similar groups of the target population until no new problem areas were surfacing. Adkins (1974) says of this procedure:

> By checking and double-checking with several groups, the staff of interviewers obtains a sense of the importance of specific problems, the frequency with which they are shared by persons with different and similar characteristics (p. 517).

RECON Setting. RECON interviews were conducted in several churches and daycare centers located in the Central Harlem area. Harlem is a predominantly black community located in New York City. Housing conditions in most areas of Harlem are known to be substandard and the community contains extensive slum areas. Although Harlem residents cover a wide spectrum of socioeconomic classes, virtually all are surrounded by an ethos of poverty. Even Harlem residents who live on tree lined blocks, in attractively renovated brownstones and modern apartments, cannot avoid travel through unsafe, crime-ridden streets nor the sight of deteriorating buildings as they go to and from their homes.

The New York City Department of City Planning (1985), in its report on Manhattan Community District 10 (Central Harlem alone) listed among Harlem's problems: (1) a declining economic base, (2) a high rate of unemployment (among out-of-school youth the rate is close to 50%), (3) a growing concentration of low-income residents and residents dependent on some form of public assistance (the 1984 Census shows more than one-third of the population receiving some form of public assistance), (4) a low health index (Central Harlem continues to experience the highest infant mortality rate in the country), (5) poor sanitation/environmental conditions, and, (6) a high crime rate (homicide, largely drug-related, ranks as the fourth cause of death in Central Harlem).

Apparently, since 1984 little has changed for the better in the community. More recent reports (Kramer, 1994) indicate that more than 40 percent of Harlem's population is living at incomes below the poverty line. Black men living in Harlem are less likely to reach age 65 than men in Bangladesh. While the murder rate for males nationally is 10.2 per 100,000 people, in Harlem it's over 100. The area's infant-mortality rate is now 60 percent higher than that of New York City as a whole and can be attributed largely to alcohol and drug abuse by expectant mothers. Finally, no less than 63 percent of all households with children in the community are headed by single females.

RECON Arrangements. All RECON interviews were conducted at cooperating churches and daycare centers for the convenience of participants. Initial contacts to obtain RECON participants were made through telephone calls. In all, three churches and three daycare centers participated in this portion of the study.

Preliminary group meetings between the researcher and members of the target population were arranged at each site. These preliminary meetings gave the researcher an opportunity to present the research project and the RECON concept to mothers while directly soliciting their participation. At the meetings, each potential participant was asked to complete a consent/contact form, which was later used in scheduling RECON interviews.

At the beginning of each interview session the purpose and goals of the RECON, matters of confidentiality, and the right of each participant to discontinue at any time were again explained. Participants were then asked to complete a RECON Personal Data Sheet .

RECON Interviewers. RECON interviews were conducted by two black female researchers. Each had considerable professional interviewing experience with this parent population. For each RECON, the interview team alternated roles of leader and assistant. The job of the leader was guiding the group participants through the RECON process. The job of the assistant was recording problem statements onto index cards for display on the walls, grouping and regrouping as necessary. Alternating the leader/assistant roles facilitated a broader perspective and understanding of problem statements with each subsequent RECON.

RECON Sample. A total of 47 urban black single mothers took part in RECON interviews (the derivation group) conducted for this study. Selected participants were all black single mothers meeting at least one of the following criteria: (1) A never married parent or guardian of a child or adolescent, (2) A divorced parent or guardian of a child or adolescent, (3) A married but separated parent or guardian of a child or adolescent, and, (4) A widowed parent or guardian of a child or adolescent.

In setting the criteria for participation in RECONs the researcher tried to ensure that participants would represent every problem likely to be encountered by urban black single mothers. Although it was expected that poorer or disadvantaged black single mothers would present a wider range of problems, it was also expected, based on the literature review, that middle class urban black single mothers might also present problems, particularly problems related to stress level. Thus, in an attempt to gather the most diverse data possible, no other criteria for participation, other than those listed above, were imposed. During orientation to the RECON process however information regarding other variables of the sample was derived. The researcher kept track of how RECON groups were distributed along a number of these other variables in order to demonstrate the diversity of the sample. These data are presented below.

Personal Characteristics of the RECON Sample

Personal characteristics of the RECON sample are presented in Table 1. The most significant and interesting findings are described below.

Age of Mother. Mothers in the sample ranged in age from 19 to 49. For identification purposes, the sample was divided into three age groups by 10 year spans. The youngest group (19-29) comprised approximately one-half of the sample.

Single Status. Almost one-half the sample (47%) reported single status as never married.

Education Level. Reported educational levels indicated that the sample was a relatively well-educated group with the largest proportion (42%) having completed at least a high school education. Only 24% of the sample had not obtained a high school diploma or its equivalent.

Socioeconomic Characteristics of the RECON Sample

Socioeconomic characteristics of the RECON sample are presented in Table 2.

Table 1

Personal Characteristics of Total RECON Sample (N = 47)

Characteristics	N	%
Age of Mother		
19-29	23	49
30-39	19	40
40-49	5	11
Single Status		
Widowed	3	6
Divorced	7	15
Separated	15	32
Never Married	22	47
Education Level		
6-8 Grade	4	9
9-11 Grade	7	15
H.S. Graduate	14	29
H.S. Equivalency (GED)	6	13
Some College	8	17
College Graduate	5	11
Vocational Training	2	4
Graduate School	1	2

Table 2

Socioeconomic Characteristics of Total RECON Sample (N = 47)

Characteristics	N	%
Occupational Categories		
Professional	4	8
Managerial/Administrative	6	14
Sales	2	4
Clerical	13	28
Service	3	6
Factory	1	2
Homemaker[a]	18	38
Student[b]	6	14
Annual Income Level		
$5,000 or less	5	11
$6,000-10,000	12	26
$11,000-15,000	9	19
$16,000-20,000	1	2
Over $20,000	3	6
Not Reported	17	36
Major Source of Income		
Welfare (AFDC)	18	38
Employment	26	55
Not Reported	3	6

[a] All mothers reporting welfare as a major source of income are included in this category.

[b] Mothers included in more than one occupational category.

Occupation. The largest percentage of participants (28%) employed in salaried positions, worked in clerical type jobs, ranging from secretary to file clerk. Fourteen percent of the working sample identified their occupations as managerial/administrative type positions (e.g., administrative assistant, office manager, etc.) and 8% identified their jobs as professional/technical positions (e.g., teachers, nurses, etc.). Participants who indicated their major source of income as welfare (38%) are characterized occupationally as homemakers.

Annual Income Level. Despite relatively high educational levels (76% of the sample had completed high school or better), annual income levels of at least one-third of the RECON sample were not high. Thirty-seven percent reported annual incomes at or below $10,000, which is below the census bureau poverty line of $11,203 reported for a family of four in 1986 (Gelman et al., 1988). Since 36% of the sample failed to report annual income, it is not clear how many more participants might fall into this low income range.

Despite education level, it is also noteworthy that a number of women in the sample were on welfare. In fact, this finding is most interesting when one considers that education level might be assumed to be a strong predictor of income and occupation levels. Unpredictable findings of this nature, within this sample, tend to support the initial decision to include participants from a variety of socioeconomic levels and backgrounds.

Major Source of Income. Most RECON participants (55%) derived their major source of income from employment, while 38% of the sample derived major income from welfare.

RECON Data Processing

Recording Data. As previously indicated, the RECON procedure calls for writing down the problem statements of individual group members during each group session. This group recording procedure was repeated eight times. At the conclusion of eight RECON sessions over 260 problem statements had been collected. Table 3 gives some representative examples of the types of problem statements frequently voiced by RECON participants. Additional RECON problem statements are presented in Chapter IV.

Clustering Data. The process of analyzing these data required displaying all of the problem statements on a wall where the researcher could review each statement and begin a clustering process

Table 3

Problem Statements Frequently Voiced by RECON Participants[a]

Statements

---

o Sometimes I want to tell my children how no good their father is.
o At times I feel like I deprived my daughter of her father.
o I wish I could take my children out of public school.
o Schools here are lousy! They don't teach!
o My son/daughter doesn't want to go to school.
o It's harder with boys, especially as they get bigger. They don't want to listen to you.
o There just ain't enough rules for today's children.
o As a parent you have to be afraid of drugs and weapons and city life, period!
o How do you begin a social life at 42?
o People in the city don't help each other. They see something happening and nobody cares.
o There are no supports for single mothers.
o I don't have time.
o I want a certain kind of job but I'd have to go back to school. I don't know if I can deal with that now.
o I want a certain kind of job but I'd have to go back to school. I don't know if I can deal with that now.
o I want the kids' father to spend more time with them.
o I expect my children to do what is right and they know that.
o All they do is give you a hard time at welfare.

---

[a] Statements are not exact quotes but representative examples of problem areas. The list is not exhaustive.

which would eventually narrow down the number of statements and establish problem areas.

Processing of RECON data took place over a period of seven months, and coincided with data collection procedures. As each RECON group was completed, the problem statements collected from that particular session were added to those already collected and the process of clustering continued. The continuous clustering process involved placing similar problem statements, or problem statements on similar issues, in close proximity and identifying each type of problem (e.g., money problems versus relationship problems, etc.). As types of problems emerged, what was most striking, was the natural division of those problems into parenting versus personal issues, resulting in the establishment of two primary problem categories for this target group: the Parenting Category and the Personal Growth and Development Category.

The continuous clustering of RECON problem statements resulted in the identification of 11 problem areas, six in the Parenting Category and five in the Personal Growth and Development Category. According to RECON concepts and methods, these 11 identified problem areas also represent areas of learning need for the target population; that is, educationally, they represent areas around which program curriculum can be developed for the target population. Table 4, the Learning Needs Syllabus for Urban Black Single Mothers, thus presents the 11 problem areas identified through the clustering process by Learning Category (previously referred to as "Problem Category"). Table 4 is the first presentation of RECON data in terms of urban black single mothers' learning needs.

Infrequently Mentioned Problems. Over time, problem areas were more specifically defined, redundant problem statements were combined and narrowed and problem areas which were mentioned infrequently (e.g., only once or twice) over the course of eight RECON sessions were eliminated due to infrequent mention (Table 5).

The topic of death of loved ones and its effects on children is an example of one problem area eliminated due to infrequent mention. The topic was raised by one participant during one RECON session. Following that session, little discussion was generated in response to the interviewer's initiating the topic. Likewise, the issue of single grandparents caring for grandchildren was brought up by a grandmother who was not solely responsible for the care of her

Table 4

Learning Needs Syllabus for Urban Black Single Mothers

Areas of Psychosocial Learning Need Identified through RECON Problem Statement Clustering

Learning Category: PARENTING

Problem Areas

1. Educating Children
2. Communicating with Children
3. Protecting Children from Crime
4. Disciplining Children
5. Identifying Positive Role Models
6. Finding Affordable Leisure Activities

Learning Category: PERSONAL GROWTH AND DEVELOPMENT

Problem Areas

1. Managing Money
2. Overcoming Lack of Support, Alienation and Loneliness
3. Handling Anger, Guilt, Worry and Frustration
4. Managing Time
5. Planning for Career and Education

Table 5

Examples of Problem Statements Infrequently Voiced by RECON Participants

Statements
o I don't talk about death or take my child to funerals.
o I have problems with my child playing. He likes to flip and always gets hurt.
o I'm a single grandmother and I get tired of having my children always expecting me to keep their children.
o My two year old son keeps waking up nights with nightmares.
o I'm taking care of my sister's kids and I need to know how to get some help from welfare.

grandchildren. Although a few other participants, identifying themselves also as grandmothers, tended to agree, it was clear, in this and subsequent RECON sessions, that this topic was not an area of concern for most of the mothers in the sample. Interestingly, there were few topics spontaneously brought up in RECONs that fit into the infrequently mentioned category, an occurrence which seems to support the value of the RECON as an effective group interview technique. Once begun, RECON participants, taking cues from others in the group as well as from the facilitator, tend to focus on those areas of most shared concern for the group.

Significant Others. The essential and important processing and refinement of RECON data was enhanced by the continual addition of new problem statements as well as by the data collected from individual interviews with "significant others" (to be described below under 'Clinician Interviews') which were ongoing during RECON data processing.

An Iterative Process. It should be remembered that the RECON process is iterative in that the results from each session affected the way the researcher gathered information from one group to another. In effect, the researcher in this study, through this process, was learning to, ask more refined questions, get more examples, increase specificity and examine whether participants were experiencing problems in similar ways. Thus, cards collected from later groups could be expected to be more precise, exhibiting more refinements that had previously been recorded.

Suggestions for Further Study

It will be noted that the collection and analysis of the personal and socioeconomic characteristics data of the RECON sample is primarily generic; that is, the data were not collected nor analyzed in terms of the differences which might have existed in income and education levels, in single status, age of mother, number of children, gender of children, or age of children. Since the primary purpose of this study was the initial assessment of the generic psycho-social needs of urban black single mothers for their proposed use in the design of a parenting/personal development program and, because of the exploratory nature of the study, a more in-depth analysis of personal and socioeconomic characteristics of the RECON sample was not conducted. In future studies however, analyses of differences in personal and socioeconomic characteristics, such as those listed above, would reveal data of great interest and importance to the design of programs for a range of parent subgroups.

THE INTERPRETIVE PHASE

Clinician Interviews

Rationale. Individual interviews were conducted with professionals in the mental health field (clinicians), for two reasons. Interviews were conducted to substantiate and clarify problem statements collected in group RECON interviews and to assist the researcher in the analysis of RECON data; that is, to help the researcher to better understand the psycho-social problems of the target population. In this sense, clinicians served as consultants to the researcher during this Interpretive Phase of the study.

Process. Clinician Interviews began after the fourth RECON interview. RECON data was needed before Clinician Interviews could begin because RECON problem statements provided the basic material for the Clinician Interview sessions. Once Clinician Interviews began, both types of interviews were conducted concurrently throughout the completion of this phase of the study.

Clinical Interviews became an integral part of RECON data processing as problem statements and categories, derived from group RECON interviews were continually checked and assessed against the perspectives, substantiation, and clarifications of the clinicians. The process of checking, assessing, substantiating, and clarifying permitted the researcher to increasingly enter the phenomenological reference of the individual group members, to learn more about their situations and develop a better understanding of the target populations' problems over time.

Clinician Setting. A non-profit, family-oriented community mental health agency was selected as an appropriate setting in which to conduct professional interviews based on the criteria for clinician selection as well as for the agency's location, reputation, and long established record of service to the Harlem community. A large proportion of the agency's service population was composed of black single mothers and their children. In a previous study, involving 92 of the clinic's parents, 75 percent were found to be single mothers (Flintall, 1983). Hence, the clinicians associated with the clinic had well established, extensive professional contacts with members of the target population of this study.

Clinician Sample. A total of nine clinicians participated in interviews. The following criteria were established for the selection of clinicians included in the study: (1) The clinician must be a black mental health professional, and, (2) he or she must have had at least five years of experience as a clinician with extensive professional contact with members of the target population of this study. Table 6 shows gender and professional experience of the sample.

These criteria were established because it was believed that experienced black clinicians would bring a culturally compatible sensitivity and understanding to the complexity of psycho-social issues and problems experienced by the target population.

Clinician Arrangements. Individual appointments were scheduled with each clinician by telephone or in person. Each interview took place in the clinician's office and was planned to last approximately one hour. Each clinician was interviewed at least twice. The first interview took place as soon after the fourth RECON session as possible and the second interview, following termination of RECON sessions. Clinicians were asked to sign a consent form before beginning the interview.

Interview Format. Clinician interviews were focused but generally unstructured. The unstructured interview format was selected because, according to Selltiz, Wrightsman and Cook (1981): (1) It is appropriate in the investigation of new areas of research, (2) It has the ability to assist in the identification of basic issues and, (3) It enhances the researcher's understanding of how a topic is conceptualized and understood by a respondent.

The researcher found only one drawback in the use of the unstructured interview, the potential accumulation of a voluminous, frequently unwieldy, mass of data. Since the purpose of conducting clinician interviews however was the enhancement of the researcher's own understanding of the target population's perceptions, the method seemed most relevant to the needs of this study.

The focus of each Clinician Interview was the psycho-social problems of urban black single mothers, as represented by problem statements made by members of this target group during RECON interviews. Although it was impossible to effectively interview each clinician on every problem area, care was taken, in each interview, to

Table 6

Gender and Professional Experience Characteristics of Clinicians

Profession	Gender	Professional Experience[a]
Social Worker	F	20
Social Worker	F	5
Social Worker	F	30
Social Worker	F	10
Social Worker	F	6
Social Worker	F	28
Psychologist	F	13
Psychologist	F	5
Psychiatrist	M	28

[a] Years working with Black Single Mothers

discuss those areas brought up most frequently during RECON sessions.

Clinician Procedures. During Clinician Interviews the researcher read aloud several representative problem statements made by RECON participants. Clinicians were encouraged to express freely and completely their own lines of thought regarding the statements' meanings and implications for members of the target population based on their professional and personal experiences.

The researcher freely probed for clarification and explanations and the answers often led into unanticipated areas. For example, while discussing the problem of the lack of male role models (particularly for male children), a matter of concern for a number of RECON participants, some clinicians conceived the problem to be related to one of loneliness for mothers; that is, based on their professional and personal knowledge of the target population, some clinicians suggested that the complaint might relate as much to a need for male companionship for mothers as it did to a need for male role models for children. Clinicians having this perception noted that some RECON participants had admittedly been reluctant to call on available male relatives or friends to serve in this role. They suggested that some mothers might also need to recognize themselves, and point out to their children, positive role models outside of their families and network of friends. They indicated that there were many positive role models that parents could make their children aware of in history, the media, sports, politics, and other walks of life.

The essence of clinician responses was recorded in writing by the researcher. All clinician interviews were conducted by the researcher. Appendix A, table A.1, presents examples of clinician responses to representative problem statements read to them.

Throughout the interviews, the aim was to enhance the researcher's understanding of issues brought up during RECON sessions and assist in the data analysis process. Clinician responses provided not only important clarifications of RECON participants' statements but also important insights into participants' perceptions, feelings, and motivations.

In conclusion, interviews with clinicians regarding the perceptions of RECON participants were not only important in clarifying and substantiating problem statements but also in supporting the notions of this and other researchers that psycho-social problems of parents have an impact on parenting. Consistently, in their interpretations of mothers' statements, clinicians spoke of the self development of the single parent. They speculated that, given the major responsibilities of parenting alone, and the stress of urban living, if a single mother were unable to meet her own needs, it could interfere with her ability to meet her children's needs.

Suggestions for Further Study

The concept of using "significant others" in Life Skills program development is not limited to the use of professionals, although only professionals took part in this study. In future studies, "significant others" may include family members, friends and others (including professionals) who have extensive experience with the target group, its problems and its solutions to those problems.

THE NORMATIVE PHASE

Development of the SMQ

The strength of the RECON process is that it allows deeply felt problems, perspectives and issues to surface. The weakness of the process is that the researcher does not know, at the end, how representative a given problem statement is for a particular population.

In an effort to establish the kinds of norms and frequencies needed for program design, the SMQ was developed. The SMQ consists of three parts.

SMQ Part I-Personal Characteristics. Personal characteristics of the target population, mentioned in a number of research studies on parenting, were assessed in Part I. The questions represented variables which were predicted to relate to behaviors and problems represented in Parts II and III of the SMQ.

SMQ Part II-Use of Helping Resources. Part II consists of several questions designed to assess a respondent's use of helping resources. These questions represented an attempt to assess a respondent's use of formal and informal helping resources and were included because a number of researchers, previously cited in this study, suggested an underutilization of helping resources, particularly formal helping resources by black single mothers.

SMQ Part III-Problem Statements. Part III is comprised of ninety problem statements (derived from the RECON data analysis process) which respondents were required to answer on a four point Likert-type scale of agreement versus disagreement.

It was important to keep in mind that some SMQ respondents might have low reading levels, thus, a major concern of the researcher was the development of an instrument which respondents could understand and respond to quickly and accurately.

Part III of the SMQ was derived in part from: (1) problem statements made by urban black single mothers during RECON interviews based on frequency of mention, (2) remarks made by significant others (clinicians) which substantiated or clarified problem statements made by individuals during RECON interviews and, (3) problem statements developed by the researcher resulting from an increased understanding of problem issues through the data analysis process, review of the literature and clinician interviews.

The intent of Part III of the scale is to show, by frequency of response, which problem areas, identified as important by RECON data processing, also appear to be important to a majority of urban black single mothers responding to the SMQ. The assumption was that the greater the frequency of SMQ responses supporting RECON findings, the greater the suggestion that the findings are representative of problems confronting this parent population.

SMQ III Parenting versus Personal Problems. As previously mentioned, during RECON data processing, it was quickly noted that problem statements naturally divided themselves into personal and parenting issues. Further analysis of RECON data however revealed that participants appeared, based on frequency of mention, to be predominantly concerned with parenting issues. Thus, Part III of the SMQ reflects this predominant concern with parenting issues by the number of questions represented under this category. At least three times as many parenting issues were raised during RECONs as compared to issues involving personal growth and development.

It should be said that the overwhelming concern with parenting issues was not surprising since the primary thrust of the study was directed toward that area. Also, it was expected that mothers would find external issues (e.g., issues related toward their parenting role) easier to discuss. What is remarkable, is that mothers were able to discuss and reveal so many personal issues (e.g., issues that do not directly relate to parenting but nevertheless have an impact on the ability to parent) and, in doing so, many of the attitudes, feelings and perceptions held in regard to their life circumstances. The researcher attributes these remarkable disclosures to the Life Skills Model's methods which inherently provide for the revelation of psycho-social functioning of its target groups.

To arrive at a decision about which problem statements were specifically related to the Parenting Category versus the Personal Growth and Development Category, two trained, independent raters, with Master's degrees in Social Work and extensive experience in working with the target population of the study, rated each statement in terms of its relatedness to those two categories. In instances of disagreement between raters, a third independent rater, with similar training, background and experience, made the final decision. Of the ninety problem statements comprising Part III of the SMQ, raters were unable to clearly define four statements as belonging exclusively to one or the other of the two categories. These four problem statements are therefore included under both the Parenting and the Personal Growth and Development categories (tables B.1 and B.2, Appendix B).

SMQ Data Collection

SMQ arrangements. Community day care centers and churches in the Central Harlem area, other than those used for the RECON sample, were contacted by telephone to solicit assistance in locating black single mothers who would be willing to complete the questionnaire. Additional contacts were made through contacts with self-help community organizations and personal friends and colleagues.

The same criteria were used for selection of the SMQ sample as was used for selection of the RECON sample. Although there were no attempts made to exactly duplicate the RECON sample, it was expected that by using the same selection criteria, and soliciting respondents from the same geographic area, that a similar urban black single mother sample population would be found; that is, a sample which would be roughly comparable in personal and socioeconomic characteristics to the RECON sample. The reasons for wanting a comparable sample of course were to accomplish the SMQ's major objective of substantiating the RECON data findings.

When contact was made by telephone with an organization or individual, the purpose of the project was explained and arrangements made for questionnaire completion, in groups or individually.

Group SMQ completion. Group questionnaire completion sessions were conducted by the researcher on site at cooperating daycare centers and churches. The group format was selected to insure the completion and return of a maximum number of questionnaires as well as to help respondents whose limited reading ability might prevent completion. During group sessions, the researcher first verbally instructed respondents in the use of the SMQ, then read each questionnaire item aloud while respondents marked their answers. Discussion between respondents during administration was discouraged and respondents were frequently reminded to answer each question based only on their individual feelings and perceptions.

Individual SMQ completion. Respondents who were unable to participate in group questionnaire sessions (only eight SMQ respondents fit this category) completed the SMQ individually. In these instances, questionnaires were mailed or given to respondents with a stamped, addressed, envelope for return. Instructions for completion were given verbally, in person, or by telephone.

Piloting the SMQ. Revisions to the SMQ were ongoing throughout the last phase of RECON data processing and clinician interviews. Following completion of the RECON data analysis process, piloting the questionnaire led to its final revision and distribution form, which is shown in Appendix C.

SMQ coding. A simple numerical coding procedure was used to develop descriptive information on Parts I-(Personal Characteristics) and II-(Use of Helping Resources) of the SMQ.

For SMQ Part III-(Problem Statements), two trained and professionally experienced coders worked independently coding the direction of the response scale for each problem statement. The response scale was made up of five possible responses; 'strongly agree,' 'agree,' 'strongly disagree,' 'disagree,' and, 'no response,' for unanswered items. Two levels of agreement and two levels of disagreement were provided to better accommodate subtle differences in individual perceptions and encourage responses to each item.

Responses for each item on Part III were numerically coded from one to four based on the direction of a participant's possible response to the problem statement (e.g., negative response versus positive response). It should be noted that the terms positive and negative are used here to relate to a respondent's feeling about a problem issue (e.g., whether or not the issue is perceived by the respondent as a problem for her), rather than simple affirmation of the statement. For example, if a respondent 'strongly agreed' or 'agreed' with the statement, "I feel I never have enough time for myself," that response was numerically coded four or three respectively and was considered a negative response to that problem statement. Conversely, a response of 'disagree' or 'strongly disagree' to that statement resulted in a two or one numerical coding respectively and was considered a positive response. A rating of five was given for 'no response' to an item.

Generally, coders were instructed to be guided by their own judgments, based on professional experience and their familiarity with the instrument, of whether a respondent's agreement or disagreement with a given problem statement suggested a problem area for that respondent. Problem statements on the SMQ however were deliberately posed in a negative and positive response pattern so as to discourage respondents acquiring a single response mindset; that is, responding to each item in the same way. In instances of disagreement between coders, the researcher's judgment prevailed.

Based on the coding system just described, a rating of one or two indicated 'no perceived concern' by the respondent in the problem area represented by that item (a positive response). A rating of three or four indicated 'a perceived concern' by the respondent in the problem area represented by that item (a negative response).

SMQ sample. Of the seventy-nine questionnaires distributed by all methods, fourteen were eliminated following completion due to the respondents' identification of themselves as being of non-black ethnic origin, four were eliminated due to incompleteness and six were not returned. Data findings are thus based on fifty-five completed, returned questionnaires. Tables 7 and 8 respectively depict personal and socioeconomic characteristics of the SMQ sample identified in Part I of the SMQ.

Personal Characteristics of the SMQ Sample

Age of mother. Mothers in the SMQ sample ranged in age from 18 to 50, with most respondents (44%) falling into the 30-39 year age range.

Table 7

Personal Characteristics of Total SMQ Sample (N = 55)

Characteristics	N	%
Age of Mother		
18-29	20	36
30-39	24	44
40-50	11	20
Single Status		
Widowed	3	5
Divorced	13	24
Separated	13	24
Never Married	23	42
Not Reported	3	5
Education Level		
6th-8th	5	9
9th-11th	14	26
High School Graduate	14	26
High School Equivalency Diploma (GED)	9	16
Some College	4	7
College Graduate	1	2
Vocational Training	1	2
Graduate School	3	5
Not Reported	4	7

Table 8

Socioeconomic Characteristics of Total SMQ Sample (N = 55)

Characteristics	N	%
Occupational Categories		
Professional	5	9
Paraprofessional (Education)	4	7
Managerial/Administrative	2	4
Clerical	15	2
Factory	1	2
Homemaker[a]	28	51
Annual Income Level		
$5,000 or less	22	40
$6,000-10,000	11	20
$11,000-15,000	12	22
$16,000-20,000	4	7
Over $20,000	5	9
Not Reported	1	2
All Sources of Income[b]		
Welfare (AFDC)		
Social Security/Disability	2	4
Employment	24	44
Child Support/Alimony	9	16
Not Reported	1	2

[a] All mothers reporting welfare as a source of income.
[b] Some respondents reporting more than one source of income.

Single status. The largest proportion of the SMQ sample (42%) reported single status as never married.

Education level. Forty-two percent of the SMQ respondents reported completion of a high school education. Thirty-five percent of the sample had not completed high school.

Socioeconomic Characteristics of the SMQ Sample

Annual income level. Sixty percent of respondents reported income levels of $10,000 or less.

Sources of income. To broaden the base of knowledge, SMQ respondents were asked to indicate all sources of income on the SMQ rather than just a major source. Not surprisingly, given annual income levels reported above, the largest proportion of this group, indicated welfare as a source of income (51%).

Occupation. The greatest number of employed SMQ respondents worked in clerical type position (27%). Only 4% reported working in managerial/administrative type positions. Nine percent worked in professional/technical jobs and 7% in education as paraprofessionals. Fifty-one percent of respondents indicating welfare as a source of income are characterized as homemakers in the table.

SMQ Part III Instrument Reliability

A measure of reliability (coefficient alpha) was used to examine the internal consistency of Part III of the questionnaire following its administration (Cronbach, 1951). Coefficient alpha provides an estimate of alternative form test reliability and coefficients of .60 and above are considered acceptable evidence of the internal consistency of a scale.

Reliability of participants' numerical ratings on questionnaire items was calculated first for the total 90 items; second, for the 25 item comprising the Personal Growth and Development category and third, for the 69 items comprising the Parenting category. As previously explained, because independent raters were unable to rate four items as belonging exclusively to either the Parenting or the Personal Growth and Development categories, these four items were included in both categories. The process yielded reliability alphas of .90 for total items, .76 for Personal Growth and Development items and .88 for Parenting items. Since all of the obtained coefficient alphas were well within acceptable range, it was concluded that the

SMQ III was sufficiently reliable for use with the parent population studied.

Suggestions for Further Study

As with the RECON sample, an in-depth analysis of the differences in personal and socioeconomic characteristics of the SMQ sample was not considered to be the focus of this study. Again, however, in future studies, researchers may want to intensely analyze these differences to reveal data of further interest and importance to program design.

THE INSTRUCTIONAL OBJECTIVES DESIGN PHASE

Development of Learning Tracks

According to the Life Skills Model, Learning Tracks are used to define areas of learning need, in a given target population, for the purpose of program development. Learning Tracks are identified through the process of clustering RECON data over time. The clustering process establishes categories of problems and identifies problem areas for each. Problem areas, through a more refined analysis process, typically become Learning Tracks.

In this study, the problem areas, identified through the clustering of RECON data, are the Learning Tracks established for urban black single mothers to be presented in Chapter IV.

Suggestions for Further Study

Since the Instructional Objectives Design Phase of the study is a culmination of the findings of other phases of the study, it is inevitable that additional findings from other phases, such as an in-depth analysis of differences in personal and socioeconomic characteristics of the RECON and SMQ samples, would have profound effects on the outcome of the Instructional Objectives Design Phase.

SUMMARY

This chapter has described fully the data collecting and data analysis procedures used to assess psycho-social problems and concerns of urban black single mothers. The chapter focused on describing the complexity of the study's design phases and the important interrelationships and dependencies of its procedures. In addition, emphasis was placed on understanding the unique role of the researcher in the analysis process, as well as how the researcher's ability to analyze the data was enhanced by the interpretations and clarifications of significant others. Two samples of urban black single mothers were assessed and the subjects, settings and procedures used were described. The chapter then highlighted some of the most interesting and important personal and socioeconomic characteristics of both samples. Finally, suggestions for further study are noted for each design phase.

In the next chapter, major findings of the SMQ, Part II-Use of Helping Resources and Part III-Problem Statements, are presented, along with relevant background material from RECON interviews. These findings are of great significance to this study since they support the researcher's suppositions regarding the need for a parenting and personal development program for the urban black single mother parent population.

CHAPTER III

Study Findings

THE SINGLE MOTHER QUESTIONNAIRE: RESOURCES, PROBLEMS, AND PERSPECTIVES

Information regarding urban black single mothers and the problems they encounter in their personal and parenting roles was gathered from several sources. These sources include the research literature, experienced professionals, and, most significantly, urban black single mothers themselves.

As described in the previous chapter, the SMQ was developed from the analysis of data gathered during RECON sessions. The purpose of the SMQ was the establishment of the kinds of norms and frequencies needed for program design. The SMQ consisted of three parts: Part I was designed to assess the personal and socioeconomic characteristics of the sample, Part II assessed the sample's use of formal and informal helping resources and, Part III identified, by frequency of response, the most common personal and parenting problems confronting the sample population.

The SMQ Parts I, II, and III Revisited

SMQ Part I - personal characteristics. For the sake of comparisons, the personal and socioeconomic characteristics of the SMQ sample were presented in Chapter II along with the personal and socioeconomic characteristics of the RECON sample. As the findings of the SMQ, Parts II and III are presented in this chapter, data from Part I of the SMQ and information obtained in RECON sessions, will be referenced.

SMQ Part II - use of helping resources. It is important to remember that the SMQ Part II, Use of Helping Resources, was developed because the literature suggested that urban black single mothers might not have access to, or, might not make use of, helping resources, particularly formal helping resources. This part of the SMQ was designed to examine this factor and to identify additional areas of need in the population.

SMQ Part III - problem statements. The SMQ Part III was made up of 90 problem statements derived from RECON data analysis. The statements provided the kinds of frequencies needed to support the major outcome of the study, which will be presented in Chapter IV.

Findings of the SMQ are essential to the future of program development for the urban black single mother parent population because they provide insight into the populations' psycho-social problems and needs, as they perceive them.

The Single Mother Questionnaire - Parts II and III

Use of Helping Resources

As previously indicated, SMQ Part II, Use of Helping Resources, sought to examine urban black single mothers' use of formal and informal resources. The questions focused on types of resources or, sources of resources, thought by the researcher and experienced clinicians, to be generally valued by this parent group. The questions sought not only to identify use of resources but also to identify perceptions about resources; that is, questions were designed to discover whether or not there was a sense of expectation, on the part of respondents, that use of a given resource might improve their or their children's lives in some way. As such, the questions dealt not only with types of resources but, also, with perceived need for such resources.

Questions were asked that attempted to establish religious affiliation and sense of religious belief, interest in returning to school and course of study, sources of help in emergencies, availability of maternal grandmothers for help with child care, and the use of counseling resources as well as perceived need for counseling help. The resources assessed by this part of the SMQ are by no means intended to represent an exhaustive list of resource possibilities.

It was hoped that these findings would provide better insight into some of the resources used, needed, or considered of value to urban black single mothers participating in the sample. The following presents the findings from this portion of the study.

Religion As A Resource

There was speculation as to how important religion might be in the lives of urban black single mothers and whether religion could be viewed as a source of strength in difficult times for mothers and children. Since most of the mothers participating in RECON and SMQ groups had been solicited through churches or church affiliated organizations, it was expected that religion might play an important role in these single mothers' lives. In addition, previous studies had found religious belief to be a major source of strength for many single mothers (N.A.S.W., 1987), Boyd-Franklin (1989). Results of the assessment of religious affiliation and religious belief are presented in Table 9.

Religious affiliation. Religious affiliation was assessed by asking the question, "To what religion do you belong?" As presented in Table 9, results of this assessment are as expected. In total, ninety three percent of the sample reported affiliation with an organized religion. In discussion, affiliation was defined as being a member of, or belonging to, a specific religious organization, group or church.

Religious belief. Affiliation with a religious organization apparently did not always equate with considering oneself to be a religious person. To assess religious belief, the question, "Do you consider yourself a religious person?", was asked. Table 9 indicates that slightly more than one-third (36%) of the sample did not consider themselves to be religious. This statistic might generally tend to obscure widespread religious belief in the population, however, comments made during questionnaire administrations, suggested that many respondents equated being "a religious person" with regular church attendance. If church attendance was irregular, some respondents were inclined to respond negatively to this question on the SMQ. Several respondents did however frequently voice evaluations of themselves as "spiritual." There was usually consensus that it meant belief in "God" or a "divine being."

Perspectives on religious affiliation and belief. Based on these findings, the majority of urban black single mothers responding to this portion of the SMQ, have an affiliation with a religious organization

Table 9

Assessment of Religious Affiliation and Belief on the SMQ, Part II Use of Helping Resources (N = 55)

Religious Affiliation Question: To what religion do you belong?

Response	N	%
Baptist	23	42
Catholic	13	24
Methodist	6	11
Lutheran	2	4
Other	7	12
None	1	2
No Response	3	5

Religious Belief Question: Do you consider yourself a religious person?

Response	N	%
Yes	33	60
No	20	36
No Response	2	4

or church and also see themselves as religious or "spiritual" persons. These findings are thus supportive of other studies finding religion to be a source of strength for many single mothers. As previously stated, since most of the sample population was recruited through churches and church affiliated organizations with the community, the findings were not surprising.

The findings do however raise the issue of whether churches or other religious organizations are doing enough within urban communities to provide needed supports to single parent families. During RECON sessions, the issue of whether mothers felt they received any supportive services from community churches was raised. RECON participants generally expressed the perception that their churches did little or nothing to help them. They lamented the fact that there were no church sponsored support groups, special social events, advisory services, or other types of activities especially planned for single mothers or fathers. Some felt stigmatized by their church because of their single parent status. Many said they agreed to participate in this study because the RECON sessions were described as opportunities for single mothers to discuss their parenting problems and other issues with other single mothers, and to network with each other. Both the RECON and SMQ samples overwhelmingly agreed that support groups for single mothers would be a welcome resource.

These findings suggest that churches and other religious organizations within urban communities need to take more of a leadership role in developing and sponsoring helping resources for urban black single mothers and their children.

Education As A Resource

The questions in this section were primarily designed to assess whether education for themselves was viewed by the women in the sample as a stepping stone to a better way of life. It was thought that if most respondents desired additional education, that it would be a good indication that education was perceived as a viable helping resource.

Returning to school. Respondents overwhelmingly indicated an interest in returning to school, apparently to improve their work skills and make life better for themselves and their children. Table 10 shows the response to the question, "Are you interested in returning to school?" Since eighty four percent of the sample responded positively

Table 10

Assessment of Interest in Returning to School and Course of Study on the SMQ, Part II - Use of Helping Resources (N = 55)

Interest in Returning to School Question: Are you interested in returning to school?

Response	N	%
Yes	46	84
No	7	12
No Response	2	4

Course of Study Question: If you returned to school, what would you study?

Response	N	%
Computer Sciences	10	18
Clerical/Secretarial	6	10
Teaching	5	9
Business Admin/Mgmt	4	7
Medical[a]	3	5
High School Equivalency Diploma	2	4
Business Education	1	2
Music/Theatre	1	2
Banking	1	2
Mathematics	1	2
Masters in Special Education	1	2
Accounting	1	2
Psychology	1	2
Communications	1	2
Social Sciences	1	2
No Response	16	29

[a] Includes Nursing and Medical Technology

to this question, clearly education is widely viewed as an avenue to self-development and life improvement.

Course of study. When asked, "If you returned to school, what would you want to study?" most respondents had quite definite ideas about what they would like to study. Table 10 also lists the desirable areas of study indicated by respondents. Respondents were asked to write in their first choice in this regard.

Perspectives on education. The overwhelming positive response to the question regarding interest in returning to school indicates that most respondents viewed education as important to their self-development. Most apparently wanted to study in specific vocational areas which they believed would enhance their job skills and improve their job opportunities.

These findings suggest that there is a need for more educational and job training opportunities for single mothers, along with a need for more affordable and available child care services so that mothers can take advantage of educational training.

Other Informal Helping Resources

How do urban black single mothers do in the area of accessing informal helping resources? Can they depend on such help regularly or at times of crisis? Examination of these areas were considered to be of importance and were assessed in the following ways:

Emergency help. To the question, "Do you have someone to depend on in an emergency?" seventy five percent of respondents answered "Yes". Table 11 shows the responses to questions involving emergency help. An emergency, was defined to respondents as any unexpected problem for occurrence such as a child's sickness or injury, a mother's illness, or any baby-sitting need with short or no advance notice. It was surprising that so many respondents felt that they could count on this type of help.

Who provides emergency help. To the question, "Who usually provides emergency help?" Table 11 also shows most respondents (62%) indicated that a relative was usually the person depended on in an emergency situation. Identification of a specific relative was not assessed for this question.

Help from maternal grandmothers. Interestingly, although relatives were claimed as their greatest source of help in emergencies, only thirty one percent of respondents indicated that their mothers helped them regularly with child care. When asked, "Does your

Table 11

Assessment of Emergency Help and Source on the SMQ, Part II Use of Helping Resources (N = 55)

Emergency Help Question: Do you have someone to depend on in an emergency?

Response	N	%
Yes	41	75
No	14	25

Source of Emergency Help Question: Who usually provides emergency help?

Response	N	%
Relative	34	62
Friend	5	9
Other	2	4
No Response	14	25

mother help you on a regular basis with child care?" sixty eight percent said "No." Table 12 shows these results.

Why maternal grandmothers cannot help. Table 12 also identifies reasons given for maternal grandmothers not helping. To the question, "If your mother does not help you, why?" the most prevalent reason given (35%) was, "Lives too far away." The second most prevalent reason (30%) was "Deceased." Nineteen percent of the sample indicated that their mothers worked.

Perspectives on informal helping resources. Unexpectedly, most respondents indicated that they had someone to depend on for help in an emergency child care situation. Typically, this someone was identified as a relative. On a regular basis however most respondents indicated that they could not depend on their own mothers for assistance with child care, due most prevalently to their mothers living too far away.

These findings are supportive of other studies (cited previously) suggesting that many urban black single mothers may not be able to depend for regular help, as in the past, from extended family. This may be particularly true in regard to ever younger grandmothers who live far away, are working themselves, or are too busy tending to younger children of their own. Although, in this sample, the latter reason was seemingly of least importance, it is important to remember that this sample ranged in age from 18 to 50 years of age, with the majority of respondents falling into the 30-39 year age range. Considering the astonishing increase in teenage pregnancy in recent years, it is possible that with a younger age range of mothers, this latter reason (grandmothers with young children of their own) might take on particular significance. The number of older mothers participating in this sample might also explain the relatively large percentage (30%) of mothers giving "deceased" as a reason for lack of help from their mothers.

Counseling As A Resource

The need for counseling. Since a parenting and self-development program is a formal helping resource, it was thought that it would be interesting to assess the target populations' use of formal resources. In particular, the use of formal counseling resources, since the methods and techniques of the Life Skills Model, on which this study proposes to design a parenting program, are based on

Table 12

Assessment of Help from Mother on the SMQ, Part II - Use of Helping Resources

Help from Mother Question: Does your mother help you on a regular basis? (N = 55)

Response	N	%
Yes	17	31
No	37	68
No Response	1	2

No Help from Mother Question: If your mother does not help you, why? (N = 37)

Response	N	%
Lives too far away	13	35
Works	7	19
Other children to care for	1	3
Deceased	11	30
Other	3	8
No Response	2	5

counseling principles. The thinking was, that if the target population actually used, desired to use, or perceived counseling as a viable helping resource, that this would be an additional justification for developing parenting programs based on this model.

Respondents' desire for, access to, and perception of need for counseling for themselves, and/or one or more of their children was assessed by the following questions:

1. Have you tried to get counseling to help with personal problems from a counselor, minister, or other professional within the past year?

2. Were you able to get counseling to help with personal problems from a counselor, minister, or other professional within the past year?

3. Do you feel that counseling from a counselor, minister, or other professional might be helpful now?

Tried to get counseling help. Table 13 shows that thirty eight percent of respondents had sought counseling help in past year. Eighteen percent had sought help just for themselves, five percent for one or more of their children. Sixty percent had not sought counseling help within the past year.

Received counseling help. Only those respondents replying positively to the first question were asked to respond to this question. Table 13 also shows these results. Of the respondents who tried to get counseling help in the past year, ninety one percent actually succeeded in doing so. Forty eight percent sought help just for themselves, fourteen percent for one or more of their children, and twenty nine percent for self and one or more children.

Want counseling help now. All respondents were asked to answer the question regarding the perceived need for counseling help now. Ninety six percent felt the need for such help now, fifty six percent for themselves and forty percent for children.

Perspectives on counseling. Although the majority of respondents had not sought formal counseling help within the past year for themselves or their children, it was very clear that almost all felt a need for it. Of those mothers who had sought counseling help, most felt a need for counseling for themselves and/or for themselves and one or more of their children.

Findings indicate that urban black single mothers' need for formal counseling help for their families are not being met and, suggests that informal counseling resources (e.g., family and friends), if available, are perhaps not always adequate in fulfilling these needs.

Table 13

Assessment of Use and Need for Counseling Help on the SMQ, Part II
Use of Helping Resources

Question 1:

Have you tried to get counseling to help with personal problems from a counselor, minister, or other professional within the past year? (N = 55)

Response	N	%
For self	10	18
For child/children	3	5
For self and children	8	15
No	33	60
No Response	1	2

Question 2:

Were you able to get counseling to help with personal problems from a counselor, minister, or other professional within the past year? (N = 21)

Response	N	%
For self	10	48
For child/children	3	14
For self and children	6	29
No	2	9

Question 3:

Do you feel that counseling from a counselor, minister, or other professional might be helpful now? (N = 55)

Response	N	%
For self	31	56
For child/children	22	40
No response	2	4

Although reasons for wanting counseling help now and not getting it were not assessed, it could be speculated that effective formal counseling resources are not perceived by the majority of respondents as being affordable or accessible. If the SMQ sample is at all representative of the urban black single mother population, this is a clear indication of need for the type of program development proposed by this study.

The Single Mother Questionnaire - Part III

Problem Statements

Again, Part III of the SMQ was developed as a means of assessing the perceptions of a wider sample of urban black single mothers in regard to their perceived psycho-social problems and concerns. It is important to remember that almost all of the problem statements used in Part III of the SMQ were based on the analysis of RECON data, which was affected by interviews with clinicians, experienced in working with the target population, as well as the professional expertise of the researcher. In a few instances, problem statements have been developed by the researcher. In these instances, they were included because they reflected social issues of the times or were deemed to be issues of relevance or meaning to the population. Examples are items concerned with personal attractiveness, gender discrimination, and abortion.

It was expected that the problem areas previously identified in RECON interviews would be substantiated by questionnaire respondents and, would thereby extend the evidence as to the relevance of these concerns to urban black single mothers.

In Part III, response frequencies for the total SMQ sample were obtained by collapsing the two "agree" response options (strongly agree/agree) and the two "disagree" response options (strongly disagree/disagree) into one "agree" and one "disagree" response option.

Significant Problem Statements

To determine which problem statements were significant, the researcher examined frequencies of agreement or disagreement with problem statements; that is, all problem statements showing affirmation of more than fifty percent of the SMQ sample were considered to be "significant" for this study. Problem statements were then organized under the problem areas derived from the clustering of problem statements during the analysis of RECON data. These problem areas were first presented in Chapter II (see table 4). Significant Problem Statements are shown in Appendix D, table D.1, (learning category of Personal Growth and Development) and table D.2, (learning category of Parenting). In the tables, Significant Problem Statements are further identified by SMQ item numbers and frequency of response. Problem statements fitting a given problem area, but not meeting the criteria established for significance, are also indicated in these tables.

It should be noted that problem statements are not exclusive to a problem area; that is, a problem statement may be identified under one or more problem areas, depending on content area of the statement. For example, problem statement, item number 41 ('When I spend money or time on myself I feel selfish'), is identified under the following three problem areas: "Managing Money," "Managing Time," and "Handling Anger, Guilt, Worry, and Frustration." The identification of problem statements under more than one problem area is possible because in the development of the SMQ, Part III, problem statements were intentionally designed to include more than one problem area within a given learning category; "that is, a problem statement, under the learning category, "Parenting," could fit under one or more of the six problem areas identified for the "Parenting" learning category. Problem statements were intentionally designed in this way to limit the number of items on this portion of the SMQ.

In addition, it will be noted that problem statements are not exclusive to learning categories. For example, a problem statement assigned to the problem area of "Handling Anger, Guilt, Worry, and Frustration," a Personal Growth and Development learning category, could also be assigned to the problem area of "Protecting Children Against Crime," a Parenting learning category. Although, for design purposes, each problem statement on the SMQ III was originally assigned to either the Parenting learning category or the Personal Growth and Development learning category (except in the case of four problem statements previously shown in Appendix B), it was never the intent, during the SMQ analysis phase, to restrict the handling of SMQ or RECON findings to one or the other specific learning category. Rather, in analyzing research findings, the intent was to assess how the target group's personal and parenting roles impact on and effect each other, thereby, further emphasizing the need for dual-approach parent programming. The researcher received support in the decision to integrate personal and parenting data findings from the research literature as well as from the experienced clinicians participating in the study. The consensus of professional expertise and opinion was that this method of handling the findings assured the most meaningful use of the data and enhanced the likelihood of developing the dual-approach programming proposed by this study.

Findings from the SMQ, Part III, as they relate to previously identified problem areas, and perspectives on those findings, are presented below.

Perspectives on Findings of the SMQ, Part III

Learning Category: Personal Growth and Development

During RECON data analysis, five problem areas were identified under the learning category, Personal Growth and Development. Those problem areas and representative problem statements are described below.

Problem Area: 1. Managing Money. There were eleven problem statements on Part III of the SMQ that specifically related to the problem area "Managing Money." While some problem statements related directly to a need for money (e.g., item 10), others related to perceptions about money, in regard to children (e.g., item 63), and, in regard to self (e.g., item 41).

Not unexpectedly, most respondents (80%) agreed that there was never enough money to go places or buy things children needed, and more than half (58%) had difficulty explaining this to children. Sixty-four percent admitted to needing help in learning how to better budget the money they did have. Seventy-five percent said that they knew of no place to take children without spending money. Many respondents (62%) did not think children appreciated the money they spent on them and, almost all, (87%) believed that children should earn allowances. Sixty seven percent of respondents did not feel that dependable child care was affordable and sixty nine percent also believed that children raised in two parent homes were better off financially. Finally, fifty five percent of respondents did not see returning to school as an option for them because they could not afford it.

Perspectives on managing money. Review of the significant SMQ responses to problem statements having to do with the problem area of "Managing Money," generally indicate that all respondents perceived a need for more money for their families.

Unhappy about not being able to buy things children need or want, most have problems telling children why. In RECON sessions, some mothers said they frequently bought items, such as expensive sneakers, clothing or toys, for children which they could not afford because they wanted their children to "have what other kids have."

In general, the findings regarding money are bleak, indicating that too many urban black single mothers view the struggle to keep their heads above water financially as the most crucial problem in their lives. This is especially true for those mothers at the bottom of the socioeconomic scale. For the poorest mothers, findings indicating that they cannot afford child care and cannot see themselves furthering their education, or improving their job skills, suggests that the road out of poverty for them and their children seems inaccessible.

Problem Area: 2.Overcoming Lack of Support, Alienation and Loneliness. As previously indicated, during RECON sessions, many urban black single mothers spoke about their perceptions that there were just not enough supportive services available to them as single parents. Their concerns in this area were reflected on the SMQ through a number of problem statements. Seventeen problem statements were assessed to be related to perceptions of lack of supports, alienation, and loneliness.

Once again, there was overwhelming support for single mother support groups (96%) and desire to learn about activities for single parents. There were also expressions of need for improved social lives (67%) and a desire to spend more time with other adults (70%). Feelings of alienation were revealed through seventy one percent of respondents agreeing that people don't care about each other in the city, a desire to leave the community (54%), and admissions of loneliness (51%).

In terms of their parenting roles, it seems quite clear that SMQ respondents wanted help. Seventy-one percent felt overburdened with the responsibilities of being a single parent and wanted more involvement from fathers in their children's lives. Seventy-three percent wanted help from anyone with the job of parenting. Fifty eight percent felt they could not usually count on getting help from family or friends. A sense of alienation carried over to their negative perceptions (82%) about interactions with public helping agencies. Finally, alienation was enhanced by perceptions of being racially (62%) and sexually (56%) discriminated against.

Perspectives on overcoming lack of support, alienation, and loneliness. SMQ frequencies provide support for the prevalence of perceptions related to this problem area. The responses indicate that urban black single mothers want and need more supportive services. They want time to pursue healthy social and love relationships. They want to know that someone cares about them and their children. They want help with parenting. They want helping agencies to really help them and they want to stop being lonely and afraid.

Problem Area: 3. Handling Anger, Guilt, Worry, and Frustration. There were 29 problem statements on the SMQ fitting this problem category. Based on response frequencies, 24 were judged to be significant.

The problem area Handling Anger, Guilt, Worry, and Frustration was arrived at by clustering problem statements of RECON participants associated with the following expressed perceptions: (1) feelings of displeasure with one's life or circumstances, (2) a sense of responsibility (real or imagined) for negatively perceived aspects of one's life, (3) distress or anxiety and, (4) disheartment due seemingly to a sense of failure. These perceptions were grouped under one problem area because they were thought to contribute to feelings of low self-esteem, helplessness, and passivity, feelings which could hamper positive growth and development of mothers and children. To present the findings in a clear and concise way, each of the perceptions (e.g., Anger, Guilt, Worry, and Frustration) will be discussed in this section separately.

Anger

Five problem statements related to the perception of anger. Two of the statements specifically related to anger with children, two related to discrimination (sexual and racial), and one related to the frequency of angry feelings. Based on SMQ responses, all were judged to be significant. Sixty percent of mothers indicated they resorted to yelling to get children to obey and an equal number (60%), said they often loss patience with their children. Sixty four percent admitted to frequently feeling angry. Regarding the latter, several RECON participants had discussed frequent feelings of anger for which they could not always identify a cause. In regard to discrimination, sixty two percent of the SMQ sample felt racially discriminated against and fifty six percent felt they had experienced discrimination because of their gender.

Guilt

Five problem statements dealt with the perception of "Guilt." Interestingly, only one of the statements had an SMQ sample response showing significance. A major portion of the sample (80%) admitted to never having enough money to go places or buy things children needed. This problem statement was included here because, during RECON session discussions, some mothers said they felt guilty over not having enough money to improve the quality of life for their children.

Worry

Four problem statements were concerned with "Worry." All four statements resulted in significant findings. No less than eighty five percent of the sample worried about their children when they were working or away from home for other reasons. Considering the high crime community in which they lived, it was expected that the overwhelming majority (91%) of respondents would be worried about drugs and other crime in their community. Ninety three percent of the SMQ sample were concerned about the numbers of young people in their neighborhoods who "hang around in the streets" and, fifty four percent agreed that they would like to move out of their present neighborhoods.

Frustration

Fifteen problem statements were concerned with "Frustration." Fourteen of the fifteen resulted in significant response frequencies. Nine of these problem statements are related to frustrations associated with children, while six are concerned with issues more closely related to mothers' social lives and personal relationships.

In regard to children, slightly more than half the sample (55%) are frustrated because they have problems making children obey rules and fifty eight percent by trying to make children understand their financial limitations. As was expected, sixty seven percent cannot find affordable child care. Seventy-one percent of respondents are frustrated by the fact that the fathers of their children are not as involved with the children as they would like. Finally, sixty two percent of mothers in the sample were frustrated by the perception that their children did not appreciate the amount of money they spent on them.

Responses to problem statements concerned more closely with personal issues of mothers revealed the following: Eighty-two percent of respondents felt they never had enough time for themselves. Educational aspirations were frustrated for fifty five percent of respondents due to lack of money. Sixty-seven percent of the mothers believed their social lives were inadequate and seventy percent wanted to spend more time with other adults. The frustrations of feeling overburdened with single parenting were significant for seventy one percent of the mothers and a desire for help was admitted to by seventy three percent. Finally, a somewhat more difficult feeling to admit to, loneliness, was admitted to by approximately half (51%) of the respondents.

Perspectives on handling anger, guilt, worry, and frustration. Significant numbers of respondents in the SMQ sample admitted to frequently feeling angry. From RECON participants we learned that sometimes the reasons for feeling angry were not always clear. Responses to problem statements regarding racial and sexual discrimination suggests that some of the anger may have emanated from perceptions of being discriminated against. As with the RECON mothers, SMQ mothers' anger was sometimes expressed toward children through lack of patience and yelling episodes.

Interestingly, SMQ respondents, unlike RECON participants, apparently did not experience guilt feelings regarding the absence of fathers in the homes. For the most part, they did not perceive that children would blame them for this problem. The one area where they seemed to accept or feel guilt was in regard to not being able financially to do as much for their children as they would like.

Worrying was a significant part of life for the mothers in the SMQ sample. Responses to the problem statements concerned with this issue indicate that this is a parent population with significant cause to worry. Most of the concern related to children and the effects of crime and drugs in the community on children. Mothers worried most about children when they were left at home alone. Interestingly, respondents did not express fears for their own safety, suggesting perhaps a sense of street savvy in adulthood that they felt their children had not yet acquired. It seems safe to assume, based on the above, that the desire to leave the community, expressed by slightly more than half the sample, was primarily for the safety of children.

By far, the most pervasive perception dealt with on the SMQ was frustration. RECON groups had expressed significant levels of frustration in regard to parenting and personal issues. SMQ responses tended to verify the prevalence of feelings of frustration. Not unexpectedly, parenting can bring frustrations, but for the urban black single mother parent population there are the expected frustrations as well as some that may be more specific to this group. For example, among the most typical, was the frustration of disciplining children. Among the more specific were, trying to explain money limitations to children, finding affordable child care, wanting children's fathers to be more involved with children, and feeling unappreciated. Among the members of this single parent group, the frustrations of parenting alone are perhaps multiplied because there is not a consistent sharing of those frustrations.

On a personal level, frustrations seemed to center around unfulfilled social relationships or love relationships. RECON participants had expressed a need to have more opportunities to meet "decent" and "available" men. They expressed wariness of meeting men in places like bars or clubs. Some indicated that they did not go to such places and others indicated that they had no opportunity to do so. Many RECON mothers felt that their churches should sponsor activities designed to put single mothers in touch with eligible men. Some others however said that if the church did sponsor such activities, they would be hesitant to participate because they thought some churchgoers might "look down on them" or, "get into their business". RECON participants also had talked about the difficulty of having a sex life with children in the home. They did not want to bring men home to stay over and they could not stay out all night without providing for baby-sitters or answering embarrassing questions from children when they returned. SMQ response frequencies suggests that feelings of frustration are very prevalent in this parent population.

Problem Area: 4. Managing Time. Seven problem statements on the SMQ related to the problem area of "Managing Time". Four of the seven, by frequency of agreement, were judged to be significant.

Almost all respondents (82%) felt they never had enough time for themselves, although most (65%) thought that they did have time for their children. Only thirty three percent admitted to feeling selfish about spending time on themselves. Seventy percent wanted to spend more time with other adults. Eighty-five percent worried about children spending time alone, especially working mothers. If there was more than one child, sixty two percent of respondents believed that there was no time to give any one child special attention. Although they lacked the money, sixty five percent of respondents felt they had the time to continue their education.

Perspectives on managing time. Having the majority of respondents indicate that they "never" have enough time for themselves and, wish that they could spend more time with other adults, suggest that many mothers may be feeling overwhelmed or overburdened with the responsibilities of parenting alone. Also, the fact that most mothers did not feel selfish for spending time on themselves may be an indication of how little time they perceive they spend in this way. Opportunities for time, spent away from children and in the company of other adults, are necessary for a parent's psychological well-being. These notions however again raise the issue of affordable child care.

In addition to time for self, there was considerable concern voiced in RECONs about children spending too much time alone. Seemingly, this concern was primarily related to fears for children's safety from external factors such as crime in the neighborhood. Some mothers spoke proudly of "latchkey" children who could be "trusted to go straight home from school and not open the door to anyone". SMQ responses suggest similar concerns. In regard to time, it seems that urban black single mothers are most concerned about lack of time for themselves and excess time their children spend alone due to life circumstances.

Problem Area: 5. Planning for Career and Education. Five problem statements fit the problem area, "Planning for Career and Education" on the SMQ.

Based on these findings, educational and career aspirations were high among respondents. A full ninety three percent indicated that they consider education the "key to success," while eighty two percent stated that they had definite ideas about what they wanted in terms of career or educational development. Despite these aspirations however slightly more than half (55%) of the sample felt that continuing their education at the present time was impossible due to costs. Not surprisingly, eighty seven percent of respondents considered their age to be a reason frequently given during RECON sessions. The RECON group age range was 19 to 49 and the SMQ group ranged in age between 18 and 50.

Perspectives on planning for career and education. Having ninety three percent of the SMQ sample value education as "the key to success" indicated high career and educational aspirations. These aspirations are somewhat deflated however because more than half the respondents say they cannot afford to go back to school and a much larger percentage thinks themselves too old to go back to school.

Despite the overall age range of both groups, the largest percentage of RECON participants were in the 19 to 29 year old range, while the largest percentage of SMQ respondents were in the 30 to 39 year range. Neither age range seems "too old" to think about continuing schooling, thus, this response could cause one to speculate that the perception of being "too old" for school reflects other feelings about themselves. Feelings of low self-esteem, insecurity, or inability to cope may be masked by this particular response.

Learning Category: Parenting

In RECON analysis, six problem areas were identified under the problem category of Parenting. Those problem areas and their representative problem statement on the SMQ III are presented below.

Problem Area: 1. Educating Children. One of the most important parenting concerns among RECON and SMQ mothers was whether or not their children were doing well in school and whether or not the public school system, in which virtually all of their children were enrolled, was providing their children with quality education. These parents valued education, as previously indicated, and generally, according to RECON participants, tended to believe that their children could expect the best from life if they were educated.

Ten problem statements on the SMQ attempted to assess perceptions in this area. These problem statements examined the importance of homework, how school failure was perceived and handled, how mothers felt about their own ability to affect the schools, the value of good study habits and the influence or impact of TV in regard to education. Other relevant areas assessed were discipline in the schools, and how schooling was viewed in terms of family priorities, specifically in terms of the need for money.

First, as expected more than one-half (56%) of the sample disagreed that the New York City public school system did a good job of educating their children and, almost all (93%) felt the schools failed miserably at disciplining children. Fortunately, however, seventy five percent felt that there were things they could do to make the schools do a better job. RECON participants had been very vocal in this regard, generally indicating they were as active in their children's schooling as they could be. Even working mothers, said they took time off from work to visit the school if they needed to make a complaint, talk to a teacher, or settle a problem. Some non-working mothers said they were involved in other kinds of school activities like volunteering to go on school trips or monitoring school entrances.

No less than eighty percent of SMQ respondents expected their school age children to come home with homework assignments daily and (75%) of parents believed that their children needed help in learning how to study. Ninety three percent of the mothers in the SMQ sample did not think watching TV and doing homework at the same time a good idea. In regard to TV viewing generally, however, sixty four percent of mothers did admit that they pretty much let children select whatever they wanted to watch on TV.

Unlike RECON participants, SMQ respondents (60%) displayed a surprisingly liberal attitude toward school failure, saying that they would not automatically assume a child lazy for failing in school, nor would they punish a child for failure (69%). On the other hand, fifty three percent thought children could be expected to earn money while in school.

Perspectives on educating children. As previously indicated, education was an important and valued concept for this parent population. Education was apparently valued by mothers for themselves and their children. Nearly all of the RECON and SMQ children attended New York City public schools and both groups thought the schools were not adequate. Although their responses suggested that they knew how to help the schools do a better job, they were not assessed as to what they specifically would do. In RECONs, the researcher received little feedback suggesting that such efforts would be organized or structured in anyway.

Few RECON mothers appeared to recognize the value of TV as an educational tool or medium and SMQ mothers were similar, agreeing that they usually let children select what they wanted to watch. Since TV can be a powerful educational tool and, because children spend so much of their time watching it, parents and children alike could benefit from learning how to use TV appropriately as an educational resource as well as a source of entertainment.

The SMQ sample's seemingly liberal attitude regarding school failure differed from the RECON sample. Many of the RECON participants indicated that they punished school failure and that they frequently felt, when a child failed in school, that it was because they did not work or study hard enough. They felt this way even though they said the schools were not that good.

Money being a problem for most families, it was not surprising that many mothers in both samples thought that school age children could earn money for the household while going to school. Apparently, although schooling is valued, for some families, earning additional income takes priority.

Problem Area: 2. Communicating with Children. During RECON sessions, the subject of communicating with children came up frequently. Some RECON participants complained bitterly about the difficulty in communicating with adolescent children. Others, with younger children, said they sometimes "tuned out" when their children talked to them or, sometimes, pretended to listen. Although they felt some guilt about both behaviors, they admitted that there were times when they just did not feel like listening and sometime it seemed as if the kids "talked all the time."

Fifteen problem statements on the SMQ attempted to assess the area of communication with children. Problem statements regarding sex were included in this category since it seemed important to know if, and how, this parent population communicated with children about sex.

In regard to communicating with teenagers, most SMQ respondents (62%) believed that teens were difficult to talk to. An equal number of respondents (62%) also believed that teenagers did not talk much with their parents. As previously mentioned, many of the SMQ mothers had agreed that it was hard to make children understand they could not have everything they wanted and sixty percent had admitted to yelling to get cooperation from children. Only a small percentage of respondents (27%) took the attitude that "children should be seen and not heard" and less than half (45%) agreed that their children talked too much. Instead the overwhelming majority (98%) of SMQ mothers responded affirmatively that they believed in talking to their children about their (the mother's) feelings and beliefs and eighty nine percent felt their children knew what they (the mothers) expected of them. Seventy-six percent felt they should talk to children about their fathers, even if they had nothing good to say about them. Finally, an overwhelming ninety four percent of urban black single mothers responding to the SMQ said that they found many of the things their children talked about interesting.

In regard to communicating with children about sex, the SMQ sample seemed to be very enlightened. Ninety-six percent responded that small children's questions about sex should not be ignored and ninety eight percent agreed that children need to be taught about sex and their own sexual development. When it came to talking with their children about sex abuse, eighty five percent of mothers thought it had to be done. When the issue of sex education was discussed in RECON sessions, some mothers said that parents needed to take more responsibility for teaching children about sex. Some expressed the perception that too much of what children learned about sex, especially in urban areas, was learned from the wrong sources (e.g., friends, movies, magazines, videotapes, etc.). SMQ respondents were assessed on this issue and seventy five percent agreed. Although the majority of both samples felt that the home should bear more responsibility for teaching children about sex, neither felt that it was solely the responsibility of the home. Seventy-five percent felt that teaching children about sex was also the job of other teaching sources such as schools. Finally, a majority, (96%) of the SMQ sample, agreed that birth control information should be given to teens.

Perspectives on communicating with children. Overall, both samples of urban black single mothers seemed to believe that communication with children, at all age levels, was important. They also admitted to having the most difficulty in communicating with their teenage children, agreeing that they found it harder to talk with teens and teens with them. Undoubtedly, more needs to be learned about the ways in which these parents approach communication with their teenage children as well as about the issues that seem most difficult to discuss.

RECON mothers had also complained about how hard it was to communicate to children that they "could not have everything they wanted" and one could speculate that the degree of difficulty in discussing this topic might be associated with guilt feelings.

Interestingly, this parent group appears very open about communicating with children about sex, believing you should answer small children's questions as well as teach children about their own sexual development. They believe that parents should be primarily responsible for teaching children about sexuality but should also share the responsibility with schools. They were most concerned that their children would be exposed to sex in the wrong way, from the wrong sources. Both samples of urban black single mothers favored birth control information for teens. For some RECON mothers, the lack of such information given in time had already resulted in one or more daughters' pregnancies. Several spoke of their own ignorance as teenagers and regretted not having such information. Only two teenagers took part in the study, an 18 year old in the RECON group and a 19 year old in the SMQ sample. It is conceivable however if a teenage single mother became aware of the limitations on her life chances due to single and premature parenthood, that she would be much more likely to communicate to her children responsibility with respect to sex and procreation. It would certainly be more likely that this learning would occur if the young mother were involved in a parent education program where she could plan for her own educational and career development. Learning units could be designed to help single mothers, regardless of age, teach responsible sexual behavior to their children.

Problem Area: 3. Protecting Children From Crime. A recurrent concern during RECONs was the amount of crime in the Harlem community where this study was conducted. Participants feared their children might be negatively influenced by the drug culture and the crime surrounding that culture. Another aspect of fear raised around this issue was the proliferation of handguns. One mother told a story of her 9 year old son coming home from school and telling her about a classmate who brought a gun to school. To assess the prevalence of concern about crime, the SMQ included six problem statements which focused on fears expressed most frequently.

As indicated earlier, most SMQ respondents (85%) were very concerned about the time that children spent alone. In RECON groups, this was particularly true of working mothers who spent the most time away from home. Ninety-one percent of respondents worried about drugs and other street crime affecting their children. Young people hanging around in the street was viewed widely (93%) by the sample as a threat to their children. Despite these fears however it was surprising to see that only thirty one percent felt personally unsafe in their neighborhoods and seventy three percent believed there were things they could do to protect their children from street dangers. Indeed, we learned that some RECON mothers, working and non-working, had developed rather elaborate systems for monitoring and checking on children's whereabouts throughout the day. Nevertheless, when confronted with a choice to move out of the present community, fifty four percent thought it would be best for them to move.

Perspectives on protecting children from crime. By far, protecting children from crime, proved to be one of the major concerns of the urban black single mothers participating in this study. Both RECON and SMQ samples appear to be rightly concerned over the mushrooming levels of crime in the urban area in which they live. Media reports indicate that the mothers' fears are not unsubstantiated.

In New York City, where all study participants lived, mothers were aware that the proliferation of drugs, "crack" in particular, which had just begun to spread through the community, threatened the well-being and futures of their children. Shoot-outs over drug turf by rival gangs, at the time of this study, were already beginning to take the lives of community residents. Rapes, robberies and assaults were and continue to be frequent in Harlem and similar communities. Thus, mothers' fears for their children are very much reality based.

SMQ and RECON responses indicated that most mothers feared more for their children's safety in these urban environments than for themselves and that most thought there were things that they could and were doing to protect their children. Clearly, mothers can use further help in this area since most could not afford to move, even though one-half of the SMQ sample and many of the RECON participants wanted to do so.

Problem Area: 4. Disciplining Children. Disciplining children was one of the major areas of concern for urban black single mothers participating in RECON sessions. In their roles as single parents, mothers apparently seemed most insecure in this area. Some commented on how they used their best judgment in making decisions about how to handle situations but sometimes wished they had a responsible man to regularly share the burden. Others expressed fears that their biggest difficulty would come as their male children grew up.

It became clear, as RECON data analysis progressed, that the areas of communication and discipline were closely linked. The more open and positive the communication between mother and child, the better the possibility of effective and responsible discipline. Thus, many of the problem statements included on the SMQ to assess perceptions on communication also assess perceptions involving discipline. In total, 22 items were judged to assess this problem area.

Virtually all of the SMQ sample (98%) agreed that children need rules to follow. Unfortunately, fifty five percent admitted to having problems making children obey the rules they had set. Fifty-three percent of the sample however did not think they especially needed a man to make boys obey rules. In terms of teaching moderation and thriftiness, fifty eight percent admitted that they were having difficulty in doing so when they agreed that children did not understand not getting everything they wanted. Sixty-two percent felt unappreciated when they gave in to children's demands to buy them things, usually items they could not afford. A majority

(60%) resorted to yelling to get desired results. Despite some problems, most respondents (89%) apparently felt that their children knew what they, as parents, expected of them.

Other disciplinary areas of concern were sibling rivalry, children's friends, handling school failure, children's study habits, household chores, TV watching, reading comics, earning allowances, spoiling, trust, and finally, knowing where to go for help if you think your child needs help.

Sixty-seven percent of the sample agreed that siblings sometimes lie on each other and eighty seven percent found it natural for a small child to be jealous of a new baby. Sixty percent felt the same about brothers and sisters generally. Fortunately, no more than twenty nine percent disliked most of their children's friends. The majority (69%) did not think punishment should be automatic for the failure of one school subject but seventy five percent wanted to see improved study habits. For the most part, respondents did not feel the public school was effective in the area of discipline. Sixty percent felt they got their children's cooperation in doing household chores. In regard to TV viewing, ninety three percent of mothers knew that watching TV and doing homework was like mixing oil and water but only thirty six percent also felt that it was important to monitor what their children watched on TV. Most respondents (85%) had no problem with children reading comic books. On this latter point, RECON participants had generally agreed, feeling that reading comic books was better than not reading at all. Not unexpectedly, allowances were an important issue to this parent group, no doubt because their finances were so tight. Most (87%) felt that allowances should be earned rather than just given. Sixty percent felt that children could be spoiled by trying to give them the things that their friends had. Of great significance, the overwhelming majority of mothers (88%) said they trusted their children or would trust them as they grew up. Finally, approximately half the sample (54%) thought they knew of someplace within the community to get help for a child if needed.

Perspectives on disciplining children. Not unexpectedly, like other parents, RECON and SMQ participants set rules for their children to obey but, also like other parents, sometimes encountered difficulty in getting children to follow the rules. Unlike two parent families however urban black single mothers typically have no help in making the rules nor, in encouraging children to cooperate. It is not difficult to understand if parents resort to more yelling or, perhaps in some cases, hitting, in exasperation. Both samples of mothers admitted to losing patience with children frequently, feeling angry and yelling. Hitting children was not assessed on the SMQ.

The single mothers in this study believed that they had communicated well to their children what their expectations of them were. They also felt that children could be "spoiled" by giving them everything their friends had, but admitted that they, at times, had difficulty communicating "no" to children's spending demands.

Problem Area: 5. Identifying Positive Role Models. Participants in the RECON sample, raised the issue of male role models frequently. Some participants spoke of the fathers of their children with anger and disdain, saying that these men had not been good fathers or role models. They were most concerned with role models for their sons. A few spoke of their children's fathers more kindly, saying that these men had good relationships with their children. For the most part, however, those participants who complained, seemed at a loss for finding other suitable male role models with their circle of friends and family. Some RECON participants admitted they usually did not call on available males in the family for this purpose. The issue of male role models was assessed on the SMQ by 15 problem statements.

Seventy-three percent of SMQ respondents agreed that their children needed "a man" in their lives on a regular basis and eighty six percent of the respondents wanted "that man" to be the fathers of their children. When asked if they felt they could be both mother and father to their children, about one-half (51%) thought not.

Among the specific reasons given for needing more male role models during RECONs were: disciplining male children, taking boys to sporting events, avoiding the overattachment of children to mothers, providing a better emotional climate at home, raising the families standard of living financially, avoiding passivity in children, helping with parenting generally, and providing female children with a father image.

As previously mentioned, slightly more than half (53%) the SMQ respondents did not think they especially needed a man to make male children obey rules. Nor did most (56%) believe that boys needed a man to take them to sporting events. Fifty-six percent however already thought their children were too attached to them and eighty percent thought their children were too passive.

Although only forty seven percent of respondents thought children raised in two parent homes were better off emotionally, sixty nine percent agreed that they were better off financially. All of the mothers in the SMQ study (100%) agreed that boys as well as girls needed to learn to cook and clean and, sixty one percent believed that it was not more important for girls to spend time with mothers rather than fathers. Perhaps most telling of all was the agreement of seventy three percent of the sample with the statement, "I wish I had someone to help me with the job of parenting."

Perspectives on identifying positive role models. In RECON sessions, it became evident that the issue of male role models for children, especially male children, was an important one to the urban black single mothers participating in the sample. Despite this apparent concern however some RECON participants admitted that they did not take advantage of brothers, grandfathers, and other available males they knew, to assume this role on a part-time basis. In some instances, participants said that these adult males had, at times, offered to assist in this way. Analyzing this behavior, some clinicians speculated about whether the concern shown by RECON mothers over wanting male role models for sons might not be masking a more personal need for male companionship. Certainly, both samples of mothers had previously openly admitted to loneliness and need for more adult relationships. Additional support for this theory, according to clinicians, was evident in the lack of recognition, by some mothers, that there were already probably men in their children's lives who could and did serve as positive role models (e.g., teachers, ministers, public officials, sports figures, etc.).

Problem Area: 6. Finding Affordable Leisure Activities. There were six problem statements concerned with the issue of finding affordable leisure activities for children. RECON participants raised this issue as one of concern to them. From their comments, it became clear that many equated leisure activity with spending money; that is, in order to provide leisure fun for children, you have to take them to amusement parks or movies, etc. All of these activities require admission fees, plus travel expenses and refreshment money at the very least. It was obvious that little thought had gone into thinking about low cost or no cost alternatives.

As expected, SMQ response frequencies supported this area as one of concern to urban black single mothers. For example, eighty percent of SMQ respondents agreed that there was never enough money to take children anywhere. Seventy-five percent did not believe that there was anyplace to take children where you did not have to spend money. Eighty-five percent worried about what children did when they were alone, primarily because of fear of crime in the neighborhood, but secondarily because they could not be sure of exactly what their children were doing when they were unsupervised. Sixty-seven percent admitted that it was often very hard to think of ways to entertain their children.

Perspectives on finding affordable leisure activities. As with the need for male role models, RECON participants had admitted in group discussions that they seldom called on others for help in the area of finding affordable leisure activities for children. They said they did not know of specific resources where they could get information in this regard. Also, although they worried about unsupervised children, they usually did not design specific activities for children to keep busy when they were alone. Most expected children to do homework or watch television at such times.

Since SMQ response frequencies support the RECON findings, it seems likely that urban black single mothers might benefit from learning about resources in this area. Although money is undoubtedly a very real aspect of this problem, lack of information and creative thinking in regard to planning leisure activities appear to be equally important aspects of the problem.

CONCLUSIONS

In this chapter, findings of the SMQ, Part III-Problem Statements, were reviewed to identify those problems appearing to be of most importance to the target population. Problem statements meeting the criteria were called "Significant Problem Statements". For this study, Significant Problem Statements were determined to be those statements affirmed by one half or more of SMQ respondents. Along with identifying Significant Problem Statements, information regarding the derivation of those statements from RECON groups was also presented. Significant Problem Statements were identified by previously developed problem areas. These problem areas were originally presented in Chapter II, (Table 4). Finally, perspectives on each of the problem areas and their respective problem statements were presented in this chapter.

What we learned. As expected, many of the problem statements on the SMQ, Part III, were supported by response frequencies of the SMQ sample; that is, many of the problem statements were affirmed by more than one-half of the SMQ sample. These findings support the pervasiveness of these psycho-social problem areas among the urban black single mothers participating in this study and, provide enough evidence to support further explorations into these problem areas with larger samples of the urban black single mother parent population.

Findings also suggest that many of the problem statements, although not supported as significant by the response frequency criteria of this study, nevertheless, have high enough response frequencies to indicate a possible need in the population. It is for this reason that such statements, in table C.1 (Appendix C) are labeled as "not significant" rather than insignificant.

The SMQ clearly substantiated psycho-social problem areas, previously identified in RECONs, in which urban black single mothers could fuse additional learning and/or counseling resources. Resources, such as the Life Skills parenting/personal development program proposed by this study, which could help urban black single mothers needing services to maximize their and their children's potentials. Some of the learning and counseling problem areas identified were: budgeting and managing the home; planning for education and career; setting long and short term goals; handling emotions like anger, worry, and frustration and converting the energy expended on them into positive behaviors; developing or finding better support systems and social networks; and developing more fulfilling relationships; helping schools to better educate children; developing more effective communication with children; protecting children from crime; disciplining children effectively; finding and using positive male and female role models; and, creating and finding quality and affordable leisure activities for families.

The findings presented in this chapter are the foundation for the work to follow in Chapter IV. In Chapter IV, the primary outcome of the study, Learning Tracks and Learning Objectives for a Life Skills parenting/personal development program (derived from a synthesis of RECON and SMQ data specifically for urban black single mothers) are presented.

CHAPTER IV

Application

TOWARD THE DESIGN OF A PARENTING AND PERSONAL DEVELOPMENT PROGRAM FOR SINGLE MOTHERS

Developing Program Curriculum

Learning tracks. As indicated in the last chapter, the process of analyzing RECON data required writing all of the problem statements on 5 x 8 cards and displaying all of the problem statements on a wall where the researcher could review each statement and begin a clustering process which, over time, eventually narrowed down the number of statements and established a set of Problem Areas specific to urban black single mothers. Based on the Life Skills Model, Problem Areas derived through the clustering and categorizing process become Learning Tracks for the eventual selection and development of Life Skills Learning Units. The Learning Tracks established for this study resulted from the clustering and categorizing of RECON data.

Learning objectives. Following the identification of Learning Tracks, a set of Learning Objectives were designed for each track which addressed the defined learning needs. This process involved analyzing the problems which make up each Learning Track, deciding which of the problems appear to be resolvable through learning, and designing a set of Learning Objectives ("How To's") which define specifically what must be learned to resolve the problems.

Application of the Learning Tracks

This chapter presents the major application of the study's findings in the form of Preliminary Learning Tracks and Preliminary Learning Objectives. The learning tracks and objectives designed for this study are "preliminary" because they represent the initial findings of a first investigation in this learning area, with this parent population. Before learning tracks or learning objectives can be considered final, many additional, in-depth RECON interviews would need to be conducted. Additional RECONs could not only result in the identification of additional learning tracks and learning objectives but, could also impact the selection of learning tracks for learning unit development.

The fact that the current study's learning tracks and learning objectives are preliminary does not detract from their value, since the literature review revealed that a needs assessment, of an affective nature, had never been conducted with this parent population. Thus, the Preliminary Learning Tracks and Objectives presented here represent the very first attempt to: (1) assess the psycho-social problems of a very significant and under-served, parent population, (2) place those problems in the context of a learning program, and (3) propose the use of a more appropriate program design model for parent education program design for this parent group.

Chapter Organization

The first half of the chapter re-examines the three data collection procedures used in the study (e.g., RECON interviews, Clinician interviews and the SMQ), and describes the synthesis of data which led to the creation of the Preliminary Learning Tracks and Objectives. The second half, and most important section of the chapter, presents the study's major application of its findings: Preliminary Learning Tracks and Objectives for a Life Skills Parenting and Personal Development Program for Urban Black Single Mothers.

THE SYNTHESIS OF DATA IN THE DEVELOPMENT OF PRELIMINARY LEARNING TRACKS

The three procedures used in this study to assess the Life Skills learning needs of urban black single mothers and establish their pervasiveness in this population were: (1) RECON interviews, (2) Clinician interviews, and (3) the SMQ.

RECON Interviews

As previously described, the RECON interview is a group psycho-social needs assessment method. As described by Adkins (1974) the method is designed to help a program design team find out from a target population "where they hurt." The aim of the team is to discover what are the psychological and social problems that the individuals cannot solve and to understand those problems better from the individual's perspectives.

The data collected from a series of RECON interview sessions was put through an extensive data processing procedure, which required the clustering of problem statements collected in RECON interview sessions and the development of problem areas. Over time, problem statements were more specifically defined, redundant statements combined, and problem areas, which were mentioned infrequently, were eliminated.

Clinician Interviews

The RECON data processing procedure was continuously affected by the individual interviews with clinicians which were ongoing throughout this period. RECON interview data were continually checked and assessed against the perspectives, substantiations, and clarifications of the clinicians. This process of checking, assessing, substantiating, and clarifying allowed the researcher to enter the phenomenological reference of individual group members and helped the researcher to develop a better understanding of the population's problems. Thus, it should be added that another essential element in the synthesis of RECON and

Clinician interview data, was the researcher's experiential and professional knowledge of the target population.

The RECON processing procedure resulted in the following:

1. The natural derivation of two learning categories for a parent education program for urban black single mothers, the Personal Growth and Development Category, and the Parenting Category. Each of these learning categories contain learning tracks. Each learning track has the potential of becoming a learning unit and,

2. the development of the SMQ.

The Single Mother Questionnaire (SMQ)

The SMQ was created to help in establishing the kinds of norms and frequencies needed for program design. Although the RECON allows deeply felt problems, perspectives, and issues to surface, it is difficult to know at the end of the process how representative a given problem statement is for a particular population. The SMQ consisted of three parts. Part I was comprised of personal and socioeconomic characteristics expected to relate to behaviors and problems represented in Parts II and III.

Parts II and III of the SMQ primarily resulted from the synthesis of RECON and clinician data during RECON data processing. Part II, was composed of questions developed to assess a respondent's use of formal and informal helping resources. The questions were supported by RECON data, clinician interviews, and pertinent literature.

Part III, the largest section of the SMQ, was derived from frequently mentioned RECON problem statements, clinician interviews, and the increased understanding of the researcher from data processing, the literature review, and clinician input.

To summarize, the major application of the study's findings, Preliminary Learning Tracks and Objectives for the Development of a Life Skills Parenting and Personal Development Program for Urban Black Single Mothers, is the result of a synthesis of data collection and processing. The data was collected from three sources; RECON interviews, Clinician Interviews, and the SMQ. The application is presented in the next section of the chapter in the form of Preliminary Learning Track Tables.

PRELIMINARY LEARNING TRACKS AND OBJECTIVES FOR A LIFE SKILLS PARENTING AND PERSONAL DEVELOPMENT PROGRAM FOR URBAN BLACK SINGLE MOTHERS

Content of the Preliminary Learning Track Tables

As previously stated, the major outcome of this study, Preliminary Learning Tracks and Objectives for a Life Skills Parenting and Personal Development Program for Urban Black Single Mothers, is presented in this chapter in the form of two learning track tables (Tables 14 and 15). The style of the tables was adapted from a similar one used by Adkins (1977).

In table 14, Preliminary Learning Tracks and Objectives are presented for the learning category, "Parenting." In table 15, Preliminary Learning Tracks and Objectives are presented for the learning category, "Personal Growth and Development." The purpose of separating the data into two tables is not intended to suggest the proposal of two programs but, rather, to facilitate effective design decisions.

Use of SMQ and RECON statements, Preliminary Learning Tracks and Objectives, and associated SMQ and RECON problem statements are presented in the Learning Track Tables. Learning Track Tables were prepared by reviewing the Significant Problem Statement findings of the SMQ III. If a problem statement presented in the Preliminary Learning Track Tables was used on the SMQ, Part III, the SMQ item number is presented, along with the percentage of SMQ respondents affirming the statement. RECON problem statements are also included in the Preliminary Learning Track Tables. Although these RECON statements were not used verbatim on the SMQ, they are representative of the learning tracks under which they are identified. Finally, for each Preliminary Learning Track, a set of Preliminary Learning Objectives or "How To's" are proposed as ways of resolving the problems.

Use of clinician interview data. During the Derivative and Interpretive phases of this study, interviews with participating clinicians provided important insight and perspectives which enabled the researcher to better collect and interpret data. Clinicians were often able to perceive unspoken meaning in the content of RECON problem statements which may have gone unnoticed. These important insights and perspectives are represented in the Preliminary Learning Track Tables as brief statements under the heading "Problem." These brief statements are intended to frame the conflicts and issues of a given learning track in a context which is amenable to educational resolution.

Broadening the concept of "significance" to enhance learning. As explained in the previous chapter, the criterion for identifying significant problem statements of the SMQ III was an affirmation of the statement by more than fifty percent of respondents. It was noted, however, in several problem areas, respondents affirmations of associated SMQ problem statements were often just short of meeting "significance" (e.g., between 40-50%). In order to broaden the base of knowledge for this preliminary preparation of learning tracks and objectives, it was decided that a wider range of affirmation should be considered. It was expected that by extending the affirmation percentage range, additional SMQ problem statements could be included in the tables which would enrich the knowledge base for further study. Thus, all SMQ III problem statements receiving 40 percent or more affirmation of SMQ respondents are included in the Preliminary Learning Track Tables.

Suggested interventions. Finally, the Preliminary Learning Track Tables contain a column of suggested interventions, by code. The suggested interventions are resources aimed at resolving conflicts and issues which may not be entirely resolvable through the learning process alone. Descriptions of these suggested interventions can be found in Table 16 following the presentation of the learning tracks. The information in Table 16 not only acknowledges that some problem issues or conflicts may require additional or alternative resources to a learning unit but, also proposes some possibilities which could be helpful. The suggested interventions and coding procedure were adapted from Adkins (1977).

Order of the Preliminary Learning Track Tables

The ordering of learning tracks in the Preliminary Learning Track Tables is essentially random and not necessarily in the psychological order in which learning units, when developed, would be presented. It should be noted that the order of learning tracks presented in the Preliminary Learning Track Tables, follows the order of Problem Areas as presented in the Learning Needs Syllabus for Urban Black Single Mothers (Table 4, Chapter II).

The data in the Learning Needs Syllabus and in the Preliminary Learning Track Tables reflects the range of options for the development of learning units but, does not necessarily represent the delivery options. The number of units developed, the order in which they are developed, will depend largely on the funds, time, and talent available for program development and these factors are undeniably related to "national will." National will, as it relates to parent education program development, will be discussed in the next chapter.

Table 14

Preliminary Learning Tracks

for a

Life Skills Parenting and Personal Development Program for Urban Black Single Mothers

Learning Category: PARENTING Learning Track: 1. Educating Children	Affirmation of Problem Areas by SMQ Response Frequencies*		Preliminary Learning Objectives ("How To" Statements)	Types of Interventions Needed[a]
	SMQ Item	SMQ %		
Problem: Generalized dissatisfaction with the public school system which is vaguely expressed. Despite SMQ responses suggestion that mothers know what to do to improve the quality of education for children, comments reveal little is being done by them which will specifically impact on children's educations.			How to investigate the quality of the education your child is receiving.	1
			How to initiate changes through your local school board.	1
Associated SMQ Problem Statements:			How to initiate changes at home which will impact your child's schooling.	1
o Public schools do a good job of educating children.	14	56 D	How to get information about funding resources for private schooling.	1,2
o Public schools do a good job of disciplining children.	56	93 D		
Associated RECON Problem Statements:				
o Schools here are lousy. They don't teach.				
o I want to take my daughter out of public school but I can't afford private school				

*SMQ Problem Statements affirmed by 40% or more of SMQ respondents.
[a]Refer to Code Sheet - Table 16

Table 14

Preliminary Learning Tracks

for a

Life Skills Parenting and Personal Development Program
for Urban Black Single Mothers

Learning Category: PARENTING Learning Track: 1. Educating Children (cont.)	Affirmation of Problem Areas by SMQ Response Frequencies*		Preliminary Learning Objectives ("How To" Statements)	Types of Interventions Needed[a]
	SMQ Item	SMQ %		
Problem: Inaccurate perceptions or assessments of children's school difficulties, sometimes resulting in over-reactions or inappropriate responding.			How to get help in accurately assessing your child's school problems	1,2
Associated SMQ Problem Statements:			How to positively communicate with your child about his/her school problems.	1
o When my children fail in school I know it's because they are lazy.	74	40 A	How to positively communicate with school personnel about your child's school problems.	1
Associated RECON Problem Statements:			How to get information regarding learning disabilities.	1,2
o I tried everything to get my son interested in school again, including punishment, but nothing worked.			How to get your child assessed for learning difficulties.	1,2
o His teacher is prejudiced.			How to find out about your and your child's rights if he or she is learning disabled.	1,2
o He's just lazy and won't study.				

*SMQ Problem Statements affirmed by 40% or more of SMQ respondents.

[a]Refer to Code Sheet - Table 16

Table 14

Preliminary Learning Tracks

for a

Life Skills Parenting and Personal Development Program
for Urban Black Single Mothers

Learning Category: PARENTING Learning Track: 1. Educating Children (cont.)	Affirmation of Problem Areas by SMQ Response Frequencies *		Preliminary Learning Objectives ("How To" Statements)	Types of Interventions Needed[a]
	SMQ Item	SMQ %		
Problem: Understanding the importance of study and homework time but usually not involved in monitoring study or homework behaviors.			How to establish a good study environment.	1
Associated SMQ Problem Statements:			How to monitor homework and study behaviors.	1
o I expect my children to have homework every night.	68	80 A	How to plan or schedule time to supervise homework time.	1
o My children need to learn how to study.	54	75 A	How to monitor and use TV as an educational tool.	1
o My children select what they want to see on TV.	57	64 A	How to learn more about good study habits and teach your child.	1
Associated RECON Problem Statements:				
o I usually ask to see their homework before they go to bed.			How to collaborate with teachers on homework and study habits.	1
o I try to keep up but I admit sometimes I'm just too tired to check on them.				
o They come home and say they don't have any homework.				

*SMQ Problem Statements affirmed by 40% or more of SMQ respondents.
[a]Refer to Code Sheet - Table 16

Table 14

Preliminary Learning Tracks

for a

Life Skills Parenting and Personal Development Program
for Urban Black Single Mothers

Learning Category: PARENTING Learning Track: 1. Educating Children (cont.)	Affirmation of Problem Areas by SMQ Response Frequencies*		Preliminary Learning Objectives ("How To" Statements)	Types of Interventions Needed[a]
	SMQ Item	SMQ %		
Problem: Unrealistic expectations of children which interfere with the ability to properly prioritize their schooling needs.			How to prioritize your child's schooling needs.	1
Associated SMQ Problem Statements:			How to plan ahead for emergencies to avoid crisis decision making.	1
o I can't expect my children to earn money while they are going to school.	76	53 D	How to manage your household by assigning doable and realistic tasks for all family members.	1
Associated RECON Problem Statements:				
o Sometimes I have to keep my oldest daughter home from school to babysit her little brother.			How to avoid placing too many adult responsibilities on children.	1
o He has to have a job after school because we need the income.				

*SMQ Problem Statements affirmed by 40% or more of SMQ respondents.
[a]Refer to Code Sheet - Table 16

Table 14

Preliminary Learning Tracks

for a

Life Skills Parenting and Personal Development Program for Urban Black Single Mothers

Learning Category: PARENTING Learning Track: 2. Communicating with Children	Affirmation of Problem Areas by SMQ Response Frequencies*		Preliminary Learning Objectives ("How To" Statements)	Types of Interventions Needed[a]
	SMQ Item	SMQ %		
Problem: Having difficulty communicating positively with adolescent children and finding it hard to understand adolescents' tendency to become more reticent in his or her communications with adults, particularly parents. Wanting to improve communication.			How to encourage and promote meaningful communication between you and your adolescent.	1
			How to permit your adolescent child his or her sense of privacy.	1
Associated SMQ Problem Statements:				
o I think that teenage children are difficult to talk to.	3	62 A	How to convey to your adolescent that you believe he or she is trustworthy.	1
o I believe in talking to my children about my feelings and beliefs.	71	98 A	How to assert your authority as a parent through positive communication.	1
Associated RECON Problem Statements:			How to communicate anger or displeasure with your child without losing control.	1
o He keeps things to himself and I never know what he's thinking.			How to avoid instilling feelings of low self-esteem in children through negative communications.	1
o I tried everything to talk with them but they won't talk to me.			How to monitor what you say to your children and how you say it.	1

*SMQ Problem Statements affirmed by 40% or more of SMQ respondents.

[a] Refer to Code Sheet - Table 16

Table 14

Preliminary Learning Tracks

for a

Life Skills Parenting and Personal Development Program
for Urban Black Single Mothers

Learning Category: PARENTING Learning Track: 2. Communicating with Children (cont.)	Affirmation of Problem Areas by SMQ Response Frequencies *		Preliminary Learning Objectives ("How To" Statements)	Types of Interventions Needed[a]
	SMQ Item	SMQ %		
Problem: A tendency to stifle young children's natural verbosity due to impatience, fatigue or other emotional and physical stresses of single parenting. In some cases, this may also include a failure to understand the importance of verbal reciprocity on language development in infancy and early childhood.			How to satisfy a young child's need to talk to you without losing your mind.	1
			How to schedule real listening time for each child.	1
			How to creatively redirect a young child's attention.	1
Associated SMQ Problem Statements:			How to learn about language development in young children.	1,2
o My children talk too much.	58	45 A		
o I find many things my children talk about interesting.	81	94 A		
Associated RECON Problem Statements:			How to help your young child develop good language skills.	1,2
o You just can't shut her up. She talks all the time until she goes to bed.			How to show genuine interest in your child's conversation.	1
o I hate to say it but sometimes I do tell him to shut-up.				
o I am too tired to listen when I get home.				

*SMQ Problem Statements affirmed by 40% or more of SMQ respondents.
[a]Refer to Code Sheet - Table 16

Table 14

Preliminary Learning Tracks

for a

Life Skills Parenting and Personal Development Program for Urban Black Single Mothers

Learning Category: PARENTING Learning Track: 2. Communicating with Children (cont.)	Affirmation of Problem Areas by SMQ Response Frequencies *		Preliminary Learning Objectives ("How To" Statements)	Types of Inter-ventions Needed[a]
	SMQ Item	SMQ %		
Problem: Fearful that children learn too much about sex in the streets but believing that sex information should be communicated more in the home.			How to learn more about one's own body and sexual functioning.	1
Associated SMQ Problem Statements:			How to learn more about sexual development in children.	1,2
o Children need to be taught about sex and their own sexual development.	23	98 A	How to answer sexually related questions of young children.	1
o Children mainly learn about sex in the streets.	67	75 A	How to find age appropriate reading materials to assist in answering children's questions.	1
o I think that birth control information should be given to teenagers.	78	96 A		
Associated RECON Problem Statements:			How to locate appropriate sex education resources for adolescents.	1,2
o Sometimes I don't know how to answer my daughter's questions about sex.			How to assess what your children know about sex and correct misinformation.	1
o I haven't talked with my thirteen year old son about sex but I sure know he's interested.			How to inform small children about sex abuse.	
o You don't have to tell them anything, they learn about it in the streets.				

*SMQ Problem Statements affirmed by 40% or more of SMQ respondents.

[a]Refer to Code Sheet - Table 16

Table 14

Preliminary Learning Tracks

for a

Life Skills Parenting and Personal Development Program
for Urban Black Single Mothers

Learning Category: PARENTING Learning Track: 2. Communicating with Children (cont.)	Affirmation of Problem Areas by SMQ Response Frequencies *		Preliminary Learning Objectives ("How To" Statements)	Types of Interventions Needed[a]
	SMQ Item	SMQ %		
Problem: Having difficulty communicating "no" to children's spending demands but believing that they have communicated their expectations and feelings well.			How to say 'No' and mean it.	1,2
			How to teach children to save.	1
Associated SMQ Problem Statements:			How to involve children in family budgeting.	1
o I find it hard to make my children understand that they can't have everything they want.	29	58 A	How to learn about and teach smart consumer skills.	1,2
o My children know what I expect of them.	43	89 A	How to know if your children really know what you expect of them.	1
Associated RECON Problem Statements:				
o If I say I don't have the money she says, Yes you do.			How to understand your own concepts about money to improve communication.	1,2
o You got to give them what other children have.			How to talk about money with children.	1
o He had to have those sneakers that cost $65.00,				

*SMQ Problem Statements affirmed by 40% or more of SMQ respondents.
[a]Refer to Code Sheet - Table 16

Table 14

Preliminary Learning Tracks

for a

Life Skills Parenting and Personal Development Program
for Urban Black Single Mothers

Learning Category: PARENTING Learning Track: 3. Protecting Children from Crime	Affirmation of Problem Areas by SMQ Response Frequencies*		Preliminary Learning Objectives ("How To" Statements)	Types of Interventions Needed[a]
	SMQ Item	SMQ %		
Problem: Fears for children regarding the negative influence of street life and some peers. Mothers' fears seem to be two-pronged. They worry that children will be pressured into drug use or other criminal activity by peers, or, that children will be attracted to the easy, fast and plentiful money to be made by pushing drugs.			How to closely supervise your children's activities and friendships.	1
			How to involve children in positive peer activities.	1
			How to talk with children about the dangers of the streets.	1
Associated SMQ Problem Statements:			How to get help for troubled children.	1,2
o I worry about drugs and other street crime in my community affecting my children.	13	91	How to educate children about the dangers of taking or dealing drugs.	1,2,3
o Too many young people in my neighborhood hang around in the streets.	33	93	How to become involved in or organize anti-drug campaigns in your community.	1,2,3,4
o I worry about the time my children spend alone while I'm working or out of the house for other reasons.	5	85		
Associated RECON Problem Statements:				
o My teenage son is gambling and dealing.				

*SMQ Problem Statements affirmed by 40% or more of SMQ respondents.

[a]Refer to Code Sheet - Table 16

Table 14
Preliminary Learning Tracks

for a

Life Skills Parenting and Personal Development Program
for Urban Black Single Mothers

Learning Category: PARENTING Learning Track: 3. Protecting Children from Crime (Cont.)	Affirmation of Problem Areas by SMQ Response Frequencies*		Preliminary Learning Objectives ("How To" Statements)	Types of Inter-ventions Needed[a]
	SMQ Item	SMQ %		
o Teens around here think the streets are paved with gold and money cause they see friends with money and expensive clothes they got from dealing. o Peer pressure can make your kids get into trouble o I don't let my children hang with any children that I don't like.				

*SMQ Problem Statements affirmed by 40% or more of SMQ respondents.
[a]Refer to Code Sheet - Table 16

Table 14

Preliminary Learning Tracks

for a

Life Skills Parenting and Personal Development Program
for Urban Black Single Mothers

Learning Category: PARENTING Learning Track: 3. Protecting Children from Crime (Cont.)	Affirmation of Problem Areas by SMQ Response Frequencies*		Preliminary Learning Objectives ("How To" Statements)	Types of Inter-ventions Needed[a]
	SMQ Item	SMQ %		
Problem: Fears that children will become the victims of crime in the community.			How to network with other parents in the community to make it safer for children.	1
Associated SMQ Problem Statements:			How to advocate for safer school environments.	1,3
o The best thing for me and my children would be to move from our present community.	86	54	How to find out about available supportive resources for parents and children.	1,2
Associated RECON Problem Statements:				
o I'm afraid of drugs, weapons and city life in general.			How to advocate for a safer community.	1,2,3,4
o A lot of children around here carry weapons to school.				
o My boy likes to play basketball but he can't even take his ball out round here because the big boys would take it away from him.				

*SMQ Problem Statements affirmed by 40% or more of SMQ respondents.

[a]Refer to Code Sheet - Table 16

Table 14

Preliminary Learning Tracks

for a

Life Skills Parenting and Personal Development Program
for Urban Black Single Mothers

Learning Category: PARENTING Learning Track: 4. Disciplining Children	Affirmation of Problem Areas by SMQ Response Frequencies*		Preliminary Learning Objectives ("How To" Statements)	Types of Interventions Needed[a]
	SMQ Item	SMQ %		
Problem: Feelings of inadequacy and/or frustration in regard to finding effective ways to discipline children, particularly boys.			How to develop and implement reasonable rules in your household.	1
Associated SMQ Problem Statements:			How to get better cooperation from your children.	1
o I have problems making my children obey rules.	6	55	How to assert yourself as a parent.	1
o I think mothers especially need a man to make boys obey.	11	47	How to ask for and get the assistance of available males in your life to serve as positive influences on your children.	1
o I have to yell to get the children to do what I want.	18	40		
Associated RECON Problem Statements:				
o It's harder with boys, especially as they get bigger. They don't want to listen to you.				
o There are not enough rules for children to follow today.				
o The children are sometimes hard to discipline. Just won't listen.				

***SMQ Problem Statements affirmed by 40% or more of SMQ respondents.**
[a]Refer to Code Sheet - Table 16

Table14

Preliminary Learning Tracks

for a

Life Skills Parenting and Personal Development Program
for Urban Black Single Mothers

Learning Category: PARENTING Learning Track: 4. Disciplining Children (Cont.)	Affirmation of Problem Areas by SMQ Response Frequencies*		Preliminary Learning Objectives ("How To" Statements)	Types of Interventions Needed[a]
	SMQ Item	SMQ %		
Problem: Frustration regarding getting children to take active responsibility for household chores.			How to encourage your children to take more resonsibility for household chores.	1
Associated SMQ Problem Statements:				
o It's impossible to get my children to do household chores.	53	40	How to avoid becoming the "maid" in the household.	1
Associated RECON Problem Statements:			How to discourage chauvinism in your male children.	1
o I'd like to teach my children that I am not the maid in the house.			How to heighten your own sense of fairness in assigning chores for your children.	1
o I just want them to pick up after themselves!				
o My son feels it's a girl's job to keep things clean and cook.				

***SMQ Problem Statements affirmed by 40% or more of SMQ respondents.**
[a]Refer to Code Sheet - Table 16

Table 14

Preliminary Learning Tracks

for a

Life Skills Parenting and Personal Development Program
for Urban Black Single Mothers

Learning Category: PARENTING Learning Track: 4. Disciplining Children (Cont.)	Affirmation of Problem Areas by SMQ Response Frequencies*		Preliminary Learning Objectives ("How To" Statements)	Types of Inter-ventions Needed[a]
	SMQ Item	SMQ %		
Problem: Tendencies of some mothers to give in to children's demands and wants, even if doing so is financially detrimental to the family.			How to involve your children in family budgeting.	1,2
			How to discuss money with your children.	1,2
Associated SMQ Problem Statements:				
o I find it hard to make my children understand that they can't have everything they want.	29	58 A	How to encourage children to learn to save.	1,2
o The more things I buy for my children, the less they appreciate it.	63	62 A	How to say no to demands and wants that you cannot afford.	1,2
o I don't believe I can spoil my children by giving them the things their friends have.	82	40 A		
Associated RECON Problem Statements:				
o When I say I don't have the money she says, 'Yes you do'.				
o He had to have these sneakers that cost $60.00.				
o You got to give them what other children have.				

*SMQ Problem Statements affirmed by 40% or more of SMQ respondents.
[a]Refer to Code Sheet - Table 16

Table 14

Preliminary Learning Tracks

for a

Life Skills Parenting and Personal Development Program
for Urban Black Single Mothers

Learning Category: PARENTING Learning Track: 4. Disciplining Children (Cont.)	Affirmation of Problem Areas by SMQ Response Frequencies*		Preliminary Learning Objectives ("How To" Statements)	Types of Interventions Needed[a]
	SMQ Item	SMQ %		
Problem: Lack of information and misconceptions, particularly among inexperienced mothers, of the stages of child development and what should be expected of children at different ages.			How to understand and recognize your child's behaviors at different stages of his/her development.	1,2
Associated SMQ Problem Statements:			How to encourage closeness and affection between siblings at any age.	1,2
o My children sometimes tattle or lie on each other.	15	67 A	How to discourage tattling and lying behaviors.	1,2
o It's natural for brothers and sisters to be jealous of each other.	25	60 A	How to discourage and eliminate destructive behaviors in young children.	1,2
Associated RECON Problem Statements:				
o My two year old is so jealous of the new baby that he scratches and hits him.			How to get help in recognizing if your child's behaviors are out of the "normal" range and what to do about it.	1,2
o My daughter is always tattling and lying on my son.				
o My twenty-one year old daughter is still jealous of her younger sister. This is going on since the youngest was born.				

*SMQ Problem Statements affirmed by 40% or more of SMQ respondents.
[a]Refer to Code Sheet - Table 16

Table 14

Preliminary Learning Tracks

for a

Life Skills Parenting and Personal Development Program
for Urban Black Single Mothers

Learning Category: PARENTING Learning Track: 5. Identifying Positive Role Models	Affirmation of Problem Areas by SMQ Response Frequencies*		Preliminary Learning Objectives ("How To" Statements)	Types of Inter-ventions Needed[a]
	SMQ Item	SMQ %		
Problem: Considerable concern over the lack of full-time male role models, particularly for male children.			How to recognize and identify the many positive role models in your child's life.	1
Associated SMQ Problem Statements:			How to find ways of exposing your child to positive role models.	1
o My children need a man in their lives on a regular basis.	4	73 A		
o I think mothers especially need a man to make boys obey.	11	47 A	How to ask for the assistance of people you know to serve as role models for your children.	1
o I sometimes feel guilty about my children not being with their father.	12	44 A	How to help children identify their own positive role models.	1
o I can be both mother and father to my children.	16	49 D		
o Boys need a man to take them to baseball or basketball games.	32	44 A		
o Children raised in two-parent homes are better off emotionally.	40	47 A		
o I think my children are too passive.	47	80 A		

***SMQ Problem Statements affirmed by 40% or more of SMQ respondents.**
[a]**Refer to Code Sheet - Table 16**

Table 14

Preliminary Learning Tracks

for a

Life Skills Parenting and Personal Development Program
for Urban Black Single Mothers

Learning Category: PARENTING Learning Track: 5. Identifying Positive Role Models (Cont.)	Affirmation of Problem Areas by SMQ Response Frequencies *		Preliminary Learning Objectives ("How To" Statements)	Types of Interventions Needed[a]
	SMQ Item	SMQ %		
Associated RECON Problem Statements: o My son needs emotional stability. I am not sure that he will have that with just his mother. o He only has his sisters and me for models. o I took my son out of parochial school and put him back in public school because there were too many female teachers in parochial school.				

*SMQ Problem Statements affirmed by 40% or more of SMQ respondents.
[a]Refer to Code Sheet - Table 16

Table 14

Preliminary Learning Tracks

for a

Life Skills Parenting and Personal Development Program for Urban Black Single Mothers

Learning Category: PARENTING Learning Track: 5. Identifying Positive Role Models (Cont.)	Affirmation of Problem Areas by SMQ Response Frequencies*		Preliminary Learning Objectives ("How To" Statements)	Types of Interventions Needed[a]
	SMQ Item	SMQ %		
Problem: At times, an inability to recognize or utilize all available positive role models for children of both sexes.				
Associated SMQ Problem Statements:				
o I wish my children's father was more involved in their lives.	37	71 A		
o I wish I had someone to help me with the job of parenting.	50	73 A		
o It's more important for girls to spend time with their mothers than with their fathers.	88	61 D		
Associated RECON Problem Statements:				
o My brother sometimes spends time with my son but he leaves my daughter out.				
o The adjustment was hard for my daughter because she had no male figure in her life.				

***SMQ Problem Statements affirmed by 40% or more of SMQ respondents.**

[a]Refer to Code Sheet - Table 16

Table 14

Preliminary Learning Tracks

for a

Life Skills Parenting and Personal Development Program for Urban Black Single Mothers

Learning Category: PARENTING Learning Track: 6. Finding Affordable Leisure Activities	Affirmation of Problem Areas by SMQ Response Frequencies*		Preliminary Learning Objectives ("How To" Statements)	Types of Interventions Needed[a]
	SMQ Item	SMQ %		
Problem: Difficulty identifying and planning simple and inexpensive ways to spend leisure time with children.			How to find out about free or inexpensive leisure activities for your children.	1,2
Associated SMQ Problem Statements:			How to develop and plan inexpensive peer activities for children with other parents.	1
o Trying to think of ways to entertain my children is very hard.	9	67 A		
			How to identify and plan leisure activities at home with your child.	1
o There is never enough money to go places or buy things the children need.	10	80 A		
o There's really no place to take children where you don't have to spend money.	30	75 A	How to involve children in identifying and planning affordable leisure activities.	1
Associated RECON Problem Statements:			How to teach siblings to compromise on leisure activities.	1
o You really have to constantly figure out what to do on weekends to keep them entertained.			How to identify and plan activities for children of different ages.	1
o Kids have different likes and dislikes. They're hard to please.				

*SMQ Problem Statements affirmed by 40% or more of SMQ respondents.

[a]Refer to Code Sheet - Table 16

Table 15

Preliminary Learning Tracks

for a

Life Skills Parenting and Personal Development Program for Urban Black Single Mothers

Learning Category: PERSONAL GROWTH AND DEVELOPMENT Learning Track: 1. Managing Money	Affirmation of Problem Areas by SMQ Response Frequencies*		Preliminary Learning Objectives ("How To" Statements)	Types of Interventions Needed[a]
	SMQ Item	SMQ %		
Problem: A lack of money being an overwhelming problem for nearly all mothers, regardless of income, many are having difficulty coping with the stress of trying to make ends meet.			How to identify additional ways of earning income.	1
			How to gather information about available resources.	1
Associated SMQ Problem Statements:			How to locate and use available community resources to help your budget - such as housing, food, legal and medical services.	1
o There is never enough money to go places or buy things the children need.	10	80 A		
o Children raised in two-parent homes are better off financially.	44	69 A	How to most effectively budget available monies.	1
o I could use help in learning to budget my money better.	55	64 A	How to petition for needed changes within the system.	1,3
o Finding dependable childcare that I can afford is almost impossible.	28	67 A	How to ask for help.	1
o I can't consider continuing my education now because I can't afford it.	65	55 A	How to find out about free education and career opportunities.	1,2

*SMQ Problem Statements affirmed by 40% or more of SMQ respondents.
[a]Refer to Code Sheet - Table 16

Table 15

Preliminary Learning Tracks

for a

Life Skills Parenting and Personal Development Program
for Urban Black Single Mothers

Learning Category: PERSONAL GROWTH AND DEVELOPMENT Learning Track: 1. Managing Money (cont.)	Affirmation of Problem Areas by SMQ Response Frequencies*		Preliminary Learning Objectives ("How To" Statements)	Types of Interventions Needed[a]
	SMQ Item	SMQ %		
o There's really no place to take children where you don't have to spend money.	30	75 A	How to network with other mothers to share babysitting responsibilities and information.	1
o I can't expect my children to earn money while they are going to school.	76	53 D	How to find out about free or inexpensive activities for children.	1
Associated RECON Problem Statements:			How to avoid having children become overly responsible for assisting the family financially.	1
o I worry all the time just about how to feed and cloth and keep a roof over our heads.			How to behaviorally handle the bureaucracy encountered in public social service agencies.	1
o I hate being on welfare.			How to psychologically handle the bureaucracy encountered in public social service agencies.	1
o Trying to figure out how to manipulate this little bit of money is mentally and physically exhausting.			How to schedule time more effectively to prevent physical exhaustion.	1
o I'm sick and tired of living in a roach-infested apartment and welfare won't rehouse us.				

*SMQ Problem Statements affirmed by 40% or more of SMQ respondents.
[a]Refer to Code Sheet - Table 16

Table 15

Preliminary Learning Tracks

for a

Life Skills Parenting and Personal Development Program for Urban Black Single Mothers

Learning Category: PERSONAL GROWTH AND DEVELOPMENT Learning Track: 1. Managing Money (cont.)	Affirmation of Problem Areas by SMQ Response Frequencies*		Preliminary Learning Objectives ("How To" Statements)	Types of Interventions Needed[a]
	SMQ Item	SMQ %		
Problem: Despite money difficulties, a tendency to often overspend, especially on children's items, because it's hard to say 'no'. Overspending is possibly motivated by guilt and frequently results in feeling unappreciated.			How to be honest with yourself about money limitations.	1
			How to be honest with your children about money limitations.	1
Associated SMQ Problem Statements: o I find it hard to make my children understand that they can't have everything they want.	29	58 A	How to rid yourself of guilt about not having money to buy everything your children want.	1,2
o The more things I buy for my children, the less they appreciate it.	63	62 A	How to stop using money to buy your children's approval and love.	1,2
Associated RECON Problem Statements: o I spoiled them by giving them so much that now they expect too much. o When I say I don't have the money she says, Yes you do. o You got to give them what other children have.				

*SMQ Problem Statements affirmed by 40% or more of SMQ respondents.
[a]Refer to Code Sheet - Table 16

Table 15

Preliminary Learning Tracks

for a

Life Skills Parenting and Personal Development Program
for Urban Black Single Mothers

Learning Category: PERSONAL GROWTH AND DEVELOPMENT Learning Track: 2. Overcoming Lack of Support, Alienation and Loneliness	Affirmation of Problem Areas by SMQ Response Frequencies*		Preliminary Learning Objectives ("How To" Statements)	Types of Interventions Needed[a]
	SMQ Item	SMQ %		
Problem: Feelings of isolation or alienation due to the complexities of inner city life and inadequate support networks. Although there is an expressed desire to participate in support groups and network with other single parents, there is little knowledge of how to go about forming such groups.			How to network with other single parents within your community.	1,3
			How to organize support groups within community organizations like daycare centers, churches and schools.	1
Associated SMQ Problem Statements:			How to petition for changes which will effect single parent families on the local, state and federal levels.	1,4
o I can usually count on getting help from family or friends.	8	58 D		
o Support groups for single mothers is a good idea.	19	96 A	How to avoid becoming isolated.	1
o I often feel overburdened with the responsibilities of being a single parent.	27	71 A	How to negotiate for help from relatives and friends.	1
o I wish my children's father was more involved in their lives.	37	71 A	How to go about finding available helping resources.	1,2
o I wish I had someone to help me with the job of parenting.	50	73 A		

*SMQ Problem Statements affirmed by 40% or more of SMQ respondents.
[a]Refer to Code Sheet - Table 16

Table 15

Preliminary Learning Tracks

for a

Life Skills Parenting and Personal Development Program
for Urban Black Single Mothers

Learning Category: PERSONAL GROWTH AND DEVELOPMENT Learning Track: 2. Overcoming Lack of Support, Alienation and Loneliness (cont.)	Affirmation of Problem Areas by SMQ Response Frequencies		Preliminary Learning Objectives ("How To" Statements)	Types of Interventions Needed[a]
	SMQ Item	SMQ %		
o People don't care about each other in the city.	35	71 A	How to lower the stress of single parenting.	1,2
o The best thing for me and my children would be to move from our present community.	86	54 A	How to work at making my community better for me and my children.	1,2
Associated RECON Problem Statements:				
o There are no support systems for single parents and children.				
o We need to get together and develop groups but nobody wants to do anything.				
o You can't expect people to help. In the city there's a fast pace. Everybody has to help themselves. Nobody has time for you.				
o My mother does not babysit.				
o I would like to move to the south. In the south it's more like one big happy family.				

*SMQ Problem Statements affirmed by 40% or more of SMQ respondents.
[a]Refer to Code Sheet - Table 16

Table 15

Preliminary Learning Tracks

for a

Life Skills Parenting and Personal Development Program for Urban Black Single Mothers

Learning Category: PERSONAL GROWTH AND DEVELOPMENT Learning Track: 2. Overcoming Lack of Support Alienation and Loneliness (cont.)	Affirmation of Problem Areas by SMQ Response Frequencies *		Preliminary Learning Objectives ("How To" Statements)	Types of Interventions Needed[a]
	SMQ Item	SMQ %		
Problem: Feeling that there are no activities or organizations in the community directed toward single parents, particularly in regard to acceptable and safe ways to meet available males.			How to discover "acceptable" places to meet men.	1
Associated SMQ Problem Statements:			How to begin to feel more confident about myself.	1,2
o I don't have much of a social life.	22	67 A	How to begin to value myself more as a parent and as a woman.	1,2
o I would like to know about any clubs or activities for single parents in my community.	46	92 A	How to develop more opportunities for meeting people.	1
o I would like to spend more time with adult company than I do now.	49	70 A	How to get family and friends to help me meet people.	1
o I often feel lonely.	61	51 A	How to develop more interests in my life.	1,2
Associated RECON Problem Statements:				
o How do you begin a social life at 42?			How to find out if there are any groups or activities for single parents in my community.	1
o Churches should plan special activities just for single parents.				

*SMQ Problem Statements affirmed by 40% or more of SMQ respondents.
[a]Refer to Code Sheet - Table 16

Table 15

Preliminary Learning Tracks

for a

Life Skills Parenting and Personal Development Program for Urban Black Single Mothers

Learning Category: PERSONAL GROWTH AND DEVELOPMENT Learning Track: 2. Overcoming Lack of Support, Alienation and Loneliness (Cont.)	Affirmation of Problem Areas by SMQ Response Frequencies*		Preliminary Learning Objectives ("How To" Statements)	Types of Interventions Needed[a]
	SMQ Item	SMQ %		
o Where can you go to meet men? Bars?			How to learn to keep my own counsel.	1,2
o I wouldn't get involved with a group of singles at church. I don't want them in my business.			How to appropriately share my feelings.	1

*SMQ Problem Statements affirmed by 40% or more of SMQ respondents.

[a]Refer to Code Sheet - Table 16

Table 15

Preliminary Learning Tracks

for a

Life Skills Parenting and Personal Development Program
for Urban Black Single Mothers

Learning Category: PERSONAL GROWTH AND DEVELOPMENT Learning Track: 2. Overcoming Lack of Support Alienation and Loneliness (cont.)	Affirmation of Problem Areas by SMQ Response Frequencies*		Preliminary Learning Objectives ("How To" Statements)	Types of Interventions Needed[a]
	SMQ Item	SMQ %		
Problem: Difficulty letting go of feelings like resentment and anger.			How to discover what makes me feel bad.	1,2
Associated SMQ Problem Statements:			How to learn about relaxation techniques.	1
o I frequently find myself getting angry.	51	64 A	How to use exercise to make me feel better, both emotionally and physically.	1
o I believe that people's experiences with public agencies like welfare, social security or unemployment are usually unpleasant.	75	82 A	How to develop alternative ways of expressing my anger.	1
o Racial discrimination has not affected my life.	85	62 D	How to protect my rights when I feel discriminated against.	1
o I sometimes feel discriminated against because I'm a woman.	90	56 A	How to protect my dignity when I feel discriminated against.	1
Associated RECON Problem Statements:			How to avoid letting my resentments affect my children negatively.	1,2
o At work I get mad a lot. At home too.				
o I find myself screaming at the kids all the time.				
o Sometimes I want to tell them how no good their father is.				

*SMQ Problem Statements affirmed by 40% or more of SMQ respondents.
[a]Refer to Code Sheet - Table 16

Table 15

Preliminary Learning Tracks

for a

Life Skills Parenting and Personal Development Program
for Urban Black Single Mothers

Learning Category: PERSONAL GROWTH AND DEVELOPMENT Learning Track: 3. Handling Anger, Guilt, Worry and Frustration	Affirmation of Problem Areas by SMQ Response Frequencies *		Preliminary Learning Objectives ("How To" Statements)	Types of Inter-ventions Needed[a]
	SMQ Item	SMQ %		
Problem: Frequently feeling angry and having difficulty in controlling the expression of anger in interactions with children and others.			How to handle your angry feelings in constructive ways.	1,2
Associated SMQ Problem Statements:			How to express your anger in more appropriate ways.	1,2
o I have to yell to get the children to do what I want.	18	60 A	How to assess your angry feelings.	1,2
o I often lose patience with my children.	48	60 A	How to get help in coping with over-whelming feelings of anger and hurt.	1,2
o I frequently find myself getting angry.	51	64 A	How to help your children cope with feelings of anger, and disappointment	1,2
o Racial discrimination has not affected my life.	85	62 D		
o I sometimes feel discriminated against because I'm a woman.	90	56 A		
Associated RECON Problem Statements:				
o At work I get mad a lot. At home too.				
o I find myself screaming at the kids all the time.				

*SMQ Problem Statements affirmed by 40% or more of SMQ respondents.
[a]Refer to Code Sheet - Table 16

Table 15

Preliminary Learning Tracks

for a

Life Skills Parenting and Personal Development Program
for Urban Black Single Mothers

Learning Category: PERSONAL GROWTH AND DEVELOPMENT Learning Track: 3. Handling Anger, Guilt, Worry and Frustration (Cont.)	Affirmation of Problem Areas by SMQ Response Frequencies*		Preliminary Learning Objectives ("How To" Statements)	Types of Interventions Needed[a]
	SMQ Item	SMQ %		
Problem: Difficulty in handling guilt feelings related to being a single parent.			How to get help in handling guilt feelings.	1.2
Associated SMQ Problem Statements:			How to feel better about your competencies as a single parent.	1,2
o I sometimes feel guilty about my children not being with their father.	12	44 A	How to understand your guilt feelings	1,2
o There is never enough money to go places or buy things the children need.	10	80 A	How to assess your motivations and needs.	1,2
Associated RECON Problem Statements:			How to discuss your feelings with children.	1,2
o My teenage daughter still blames me because I wouldn't take her father back.				
o I'm considering going back to my husband for my son's sake.				
o Sometimes I feel like I deprived my daughter of a father but I didn't want to marry him.				
o Neither of us wanted to get married. I wonder if I made a mistake.				

***SMQ Problem Statements affirmed by 40% or more of SMQ respondents.**
[a]**Refer to Code Sheet - Table 16**

Table 15

Preliminary Learning Tracks

for a

Life Skills Parenting and Personal Development Program for Urban Black Single Mothers

Learning Category: PERSONAL GROWTH AND DEVELOPMENT Learning Track: 3. Handling Anger, Guilt, Worry and Frustration (Cont.)	Affirmation of Problem Areas by SMQ Response Frequencies *		Preliminary Learning Objectives ("How To" Statements)	Types of Interventions Needed[a]
	SMQ Item	SMQ %		
Problem: Frequently worried about the city environment in regard to their children.			How to find out more about safety tips for "latchkey" children.	1,2
Associated SMQ Problem Statements:			How to pressure community groups, organizations and churches to become more active in providing "safety networks" for families.	1,2,3
o I worry about the time my children spend alone while I'm working or out of the house for other reasons.	5	85 A		
o I worry about drugs and other street crime in my community affecting my children.	13	91 A	How to pressure local politicians into supporting community efforts for families on the local level and in Washington.	1,3,4
o Too many young people in my neighborhood hang around in the streets.	33	93 A	How to organize aftershool hall "watches" with other single mothers to look out for children.	1
o The best thing for me and my children would be to move from our present community.	86	54 A		
Associated RECON Problem Statements:			How to locate supervised afterschool recreational or study facilities.	1
o Teens around here think the streets are paved with gold and money cause they see friends with money and expensive clothes they got from dealing.			How to better monitor the after-school activities of your children.	1

*SMQ Problem Statements affirmed by 40% or more of SMQ respondents.

[a]Refer to Code Sheet - Table 16

Table 15

Preliminary Learning Tracks

for a

Life Skills Parenting and Personal Development Program
for Urban Black Single Mothers

Learning Category: PERSONAL GROWTH AND DEVELOPMENT Learning Track: 3. Handling Anger, Guilt, Worry and Frustration (Cont.)	Affirmation of Problem Areas by SMQ Response Frequencies *		Preliminary Learning Objectives ("How To" Statements)	Types of Interventions Needed[a]
	SMQ Item	SMQ %		
Problem: A buildup of frustration over a series of personal events and life circumstances. Although some are unrelated to parenting specifically, they will impact on parenting if left unresolved.			How to plan and schedule time for social activities.	1
			How to make new social contacts in acceptable settings.	1
Associated SMQ Problem Statements:				
o I feel I never have enough time for myself.	1	82 A	How to develop more rewarding interpersonal relationships with males and females.	1,2
o I don't have much of a social life	22	67 A		
o I often feel overburdened with the responsibilities of being a single parent.	27	71 A	How to balance intimate relationships with the responsibilities of single parenting.	1,2
o Finding dependable childcare that I can afford is almost impossible.	28	67 A	How to get help in overcoming overwhelming feelings of fatigue or lassitude.	1,2
o I feel exhausted most of the time.	31	65 A	How to handle stress more effectively.	1,2
o I wish my children's father was more involved in their lives.	37	71 A	How to ask family and friends for help.	1
o I would like to spend more time with adult company than I do now.	49	70 A		

***SMQ Problem Statements affirmed by 40% or more of SMQ respondents.**
[a]Refer to Code Sheet - Table 16

Table 15

Preliminary Learning Tracks

for a

Life Skills Parenting and Personal Development Program
for Urban Black Single Mothers

Learning Category: PERSONAL GROWTH AND DEVELOPMENT Learning Track: 3. Handling Anger, Guilt, Worry and Frustration (Cont.)	Affirmation of Problem Areas by SMQ Response Frequencies*		Preliminary Learning Objectives ("How To" Statements)	Types of Interventions Needed[a]
	SMQ Item	SMQ %		
o I wish I had someone to help me with the job of parenting.	50	73 A	How to improve your self-esteem.	1,2
			How to set aside some time for yourself.	1
o I often feel lonely.	61	51 A		
o I can't consider continuing my education now because I can't afford it.	65	55 A	How to assess your problems.	1
			How to define your problems.	1
o I think I'm too old to think about going back to school.	72	87 A	How to develop and try solutions.	1
Associated RECON Problem Statements:			How to identify resources.	1
o There is not enough time in the day to do the things I want to do.			How to get appropriate feedback.	1
o How do you begin a social life at 42?				
o When you have to be mother and father and work, you do not have much time or patience for children.				
o I'm under such stress, trying to be mother and father.				
o I don't have money or time for socializing much.				

*SMQ Problem Statements affirmed by 40% or more of SMQ respondents.
[a]Refer to Code Sheet - Table 16

Table 15

Preliminary Learning Tracks

for a

Life Skills Parenting and Personal Development Program for Urban Black Single Mothers

Learning Category: PERSONAL GROWTH AND DEVELOPMENT Learning Track: 4. Managing Time	Affirmation of Problem Areas by SMQ Response Frequencies *		Preliminary Learning Objectives ("How To" Statements)	Types of Interventions Needed[a]
	SMQ Item	SMQ %		
Problem: Seldom thinking about a plan for life in terms of setting long and short term goals and day-to-day scheduling of time. Also, difficulty in balancing work and family responsibilities and responsibility to self.			How to set long and short-term goals and plan for the future.	1
			How to schedule your time on a daily basis.	1
Associated SMQ Problem Statements:			How to schedule time for each child.	1
o I feel I never have enough time for myself.	1	82 A	How to plan special times for yourself.	1
o I would like to spend more time with adult company than I do now.	49	70 A	How to take your time and consider all the factors before making important decisions.	1
o When you have more than one child you can't give any one special attention.	70	62 A	How to set priorities.	1
o I worry about the time my children spend alone when I'm working or out of the house for other reasons.	5	85 A	How to develop a workable plan.	1
Associated RECON Problem Statements:				
o There is not enough time in the day to do things I want to do.				

*SMQ Problem Statements affirmed by 40% or more of SMQ respondents.

[a]Refer to Code Sheet - Table 16

Table 15

Preliminary Learning Tracks

for a

Life Skills Parenting and Personal Development Program
for Urban Black Single Mothers

Learning Category: PERSONAL GROWTH AND DEVELOPMENT Learning Track: 4. Managing Time (Cont.)	Affirmation of Problem Areas by SMQ Response Frequencies*		Preliminary Learning Objectives ("How To" Statements)	Types of Inter-ventions Needed[a]
	SMQ Item	SMQ %		
I'm not sure what I want to be doing in five or ten years from now but I know I don't want to be doing this! I want to work but because I'm the only parent and I've always been home, I think my son will feel I abandoned him. I had to quit school. It was too much trying to work and take care of my daughter and go to school too.				

*SMQ Problem Statements affirmed by 40% or more of SMQ respondents.
[a]Refer to Code Sheet - Table 16

Table 15

Preliminary Learning Tracks

for a

Life Skills Parenting and Personal Development Program
for Urban Black Single Mothers

Learning Category: PERSONAL GROWTH AND DEVELOPMENT Learning Track: 5. Planning for Career and Education	Affirmation of Problem Areas by SMQ Response Frequencies*		Preliminary Learning Objectives ("How To" Statements)	Types of Interventions Needed[a]
	SMQ Item	SMQ %		
Problem: Desire for self-improvement in regard to education and/or career but often little awareness of resources and how to go about tapping others' experiences to get started.			How to explore educational and career opportunities at your present job.	1
			How to get information on educational requirements for your field of interest.	1,2
Associated SMQ Problem Statements:				
o I know what I want to do regarding my career and/or education.	21	82 A	How to find out what educational opportunities and career guidance is available in your community.	1,2
o I can't consider continuing my education now because I can't afford it.	65	55 A	How to assess your strengths and weaknesses for career planning.	1,
o I think I'm too old to think about going back to school.	72	87 A	How to get help in assessing your skills, abilities and aptitudes.	1,2
o I believe that a good education is the key to success.	80	93 A	How to get up-to-date information about a variety of career fields.	1
Associated RECON Problem Statements:			How to develop doable, step-by-step short-range plans for career and education.	1
o I want to go back to school to get a job in the computer field but I can't do it right now.				

*SMQ Problem Statements affirmed by 40% or more of SMQ respondents.
[a]Refer to Code Sheet - Table 16

Table 15

Preliminary Learning Tracks

for a

Life Skills Parenting and Personal Development Program for Urban Black Single Mothers

Learning Category: PERSONAL GROWTH AND DEVELOPMENT Learning Track: 5. Planning for Career and Education (Cont.)	Affirmation of Problem Areas by SMQ Response Frequencies*		Preliminary Learning Objectives ("How To" Statements)	Types of Interventions Needed[a]
	SMQ Item	SMQ %		
o I don't like my job that much but I don't want to start all over again looking for a new job. o I would like to teach but it would take too long to get the education I need. o That's my problem. To do what I want to do, I first have to get a GED, then go to college. It would take too long and I'm too old. o I been on this job five yeats and still can't get promoted. It's just racism. o I want to go to school but I can't afford it. o I keep planning to start college every year but I just keep putting it off.				

*SMQ Problem Statements affirmed by 40% or more of SMQ respondents.
[a]Refer to Code Sheet - Table 16

Table 16

Suggested Interventions for use with Preliminary Learning Tracks for a Life Skills Parenting and Personal Development Program for Urban Black Single Mothers

Intervention	Description	Code
Student Learning Unit	Learning Unit developed for Life Skills Program	1
Professional Referral	Referral to public or private agency or organization for information, counseling, psychological or medical services	2
Changes in Community Agency Operations	Changes in policy and/or operations of local agencies which will assist target population in acquiring effective resources	3
Changes at State or Federal Levels	Policy changes at state and federal levels which will facilitate improving community services	4

SUMMARY

This chapter has presented the major application of the study, Preliminary Learning Tracks and Objectives for a Life Skills Parenting and Personal Development Program for Urban Black Single Mothers. The Preliminary Learning Tracks are a synthesis of data collection and processing methods from the Derivative, Interpretive, Normative, and Instructional Objectives Design Phases of the study. The three major sources of data collection were RECON interviews, Clinician interviews, and the SMQ.

The Preliminary Learning Tracks presented herein represent a first attempt to: (1) assess the psycho-social problems of a very significant and under-served parent population; (2) place those problems in the context of a learning program; and, (3) propose the use of a more appropriate program design model for parent education program design for this parent group.

The information contained in the Preliminary Learning Track Tables, regarding the psycho-social problems of urban black single mothers and the learning needed to assist in resolving those problems, does not represent a complete Derivation of Competencies for this parent population in the Life Skills program development process. Rather, this information is intended only as a base from which further interest will spur further study. It is hoped that the Preliminary Learning Track Tables for Urban Black Single Mothers, and other findings of the study, will serve as a source of important information in the field of parent education.

In the final chapter of the study, a framework for the design of parent/personal development programs will be described and recommendations for policy and societal changes, that would facilitate this type of program development nationally, will be discussed.

CHAPTER V

Review of Program Development and Recommendations for the Future

PURPOSE OF THE STUDY

The purpose of this study was to assess the psycho-social needs of urban black single mothers in order to create preliminary learning objectives for a parenting and personal development program specifically aimed at improving their parenting and self-development skills. The data was collected with the intent of extracting a set of learning needs specific to this parent population.

The study proposed the use of a specific educational model (Adkins Life Skills) for program development and adopted its methods in implementation. The research was exploratory in nature as this educational program model had not previously been utilized for parent education programming.

LIMITATIONS OF THE STUDY

There were several factors which limited the findings of this study. Sample size was one, both in the Derivative (RECON) and Normative (SMQ) phases, thus, caution should be used in assuming that this represents a definitive study of the population. Quite possibly, a larger sample size could change the mix of problems or expand or narrow the primary categories. In addition, both samples were purposely selected, meaning that they were drawn from a circumscribed number of community organizations, which were usually identified through their affiliation with community churches.

The fact that these organizations are also in New York City may have given the findings a unique emphasis that might differ somewhat from other urban centers. In addition, the study did not specifically delineate needs of urban black single mothers of different socioeconomic levels nor did it measure the effects of such parent variables as age, number of children, education level, or level of income, on various aspects of parenting or personal growth and development. All of these factors should be considered in designing future studies in this area. Since the primary purpose of this study was to facilitate curriculum development (e.g., the identification of preliminary learning objectives for a curriculum), it should be clearly noted that this study does not follow the more typical hypothetical/deductive design most frequently found in dissertation research.

CONTRIBUTIONS OF THE STUDY

With sixty three percent of black babies born to unwed mothers annually and, with most of these children born into poverty, it is clear that more must be done to provide the supports needed to help poor, black, nontraditional families to thrive. To do less places generations of black children at risk and an entire society in jeopardy.

This study has proposed the development and use of one intervention, a parenting and personal development program as one way of developing more supportive systems and learning opportunities for urban black single mothers and their children. The study has contributed to the body of knowledge in the field of parent education program development in the following ways:

1. It has identified and proposed the use of a new learning model, Adkins Life Skills, for use in the field of parent education. The learning model provides a systematic curriculum development process which encompasses in its design the needs, experiences, culture, and learning styles of its target populations.

2. It has applied a systematic approach to the identification of the psycho-social problems of a significant parent population and, has tried to do so from the parents' perspectives.

3. It has systematically mapped areas in which learning must take place if a problem-centered and experienced-based parenting and

personal development program for urban black single mothers is to be created (see Table 4, Chapter II).

4. It has uncovered some extraordinary perspectives of urban black single mothers about their parenting and personal development problems and their present coping strategies (see Chapter III - Use of Helping Resources).

5. It has strengthened a new direction in the field of parent education; that is, the development of parent education curricula focused equally on the parent as parent and as person.

The application of a systematic approach to the identification and mapping of psycho-social problem areas specific to urban black single mothers is an important approach to curriculum development in the parent education field. The mere existence of these data will make it harder in the future for researchers and program designers to exclude specific attention to the psycho-social needs of parents and the hardships they experience as a result of not being able to cope with life problems.

REVIEW OF SUGGESTIONS FOR FURTHER STUDY

Each of the study's design phases and the methods used therein were fully described in Chapter II where Suggestions for Further Study were noted for each phase. A brief review of those suggestions follows:

The Derivative Phase

In the Derivative Phase, further study should involve in-depth analyses of differences in personal and socioeconomic characteristics of the RECON sample.

The Interpretive Phase

In the Interpretive Phase, "significant others" could include family members and friends of sample group members as well as professionals and others who have extensive opportunity to know about the functioning of the target group.

The Normative Phase

In this phase, again, further study should involve analyses of any differences in personal and socioeconomic characteristics of the sample.

The Instructional Objectives Design Phase

Suggestions for further study for each of the design phases noted above will undoubtedly have a profound effect on the outcome of this essential phase.

It is hoped that this study will serve as a stimulus for further research and the eventual development and dissemination of parent education programs based on this model. In the next section, the steps involved in creating such programs are reviewed.

A PRESCRIPTIVE FRAMEWORK FOR A PARENTING AND PERSONAL DEVELOPMENT PROGRAM

Although the complete creation of a parenting and personal development program, based on the Life Skills Model, is beyond the scope of this study, it seems appropriate at this point to review the stepwise process, noted briefly in Chapter I, for such development.

In describing herein the creation and mass dissemination of a parenting and personal development program, the findings of this study will be related to each step of the development process actually performed. For those steps outside of the parameters of this study, findings regarding urban black single mothers will be inserted to make the process clearer. The basic organization of these processes has been described in *Where They Hurt:A Study of the Life Coping Problems of Unemployed Adults* (Adkins, Hattauer, Kessler, and Manuele, 1977), and it has been adapted here to illustrate more specifically how it would relate to urban black single mothers. Finally, in the descriptions which follow, the assumption has been made that there are adequate funds and adequate research and development centers across the country in which this process could take place.

Needs Assessment

The Reconnaissance interview procedure (RECON), used as the needs assessment process in this study, represents the first step in the Life Skills program development system. RECON interviews with groups of urban black single mothers were conducted to survey a broad range of needs and coping strategies of the parent group (see Chapter II for a detailed description of the process). The researcher then made use of her own experience and the insights of experienced black professionals which involved interpreting, categorizing, and synthesizing the data collected from RECON interviews. To assess the pervasiveness of the problems disclosed in interviews, a wider sample of urban black single mothers was selected to respond to the Single Mother Questionnaire (SMQ). It should be noted that in the actual development of a Life Skills Program, many more in-depth RECON interviews would be conducted by the research and development team.

The Derivation of Competencies

The next step in the Life Skills program development system is the expression of problems in terms of the behaviors necessary to solve them. This is the derivation of competencies process. The process involves the definition of behaviors or actions necessary to resolve the stated problems and the expression of those behaviors in "How To" statements. "How To" statements facilitate the creation of learning objectives in the eventual development of learning units.

In a Life Skills research and development center, a research team would group and categorize problems into clusters. These problem clusters, when appropriately grouped and defined, would become the learning tracks for the program such as those identified in Tables 14 and 15, Chapter IV (e.g., 'Educating Children', 'Managing Money', 'Communicating with Children', etc.).

In this study, "How To" statements are the Preliminary Learning Objectives for potential learning units for the Life Skills Parenting and Personal Development Program for Urban Black Single Mothers (Tables 14 and 15, Chapter IV). They were created through the processes fully described in the Derivative and Interpretive phases of the study, which were presented in Chapter II.

Since the data collection and most of the analyses for this study were accomplished by the Needs Assessment and Derivation of Competencies steps of Life Skills program development, what follows, from this point forward, is a brief description of the steps that would be involved if a research and development center obtained the necessary funding to design a complete parenting and personal development program.

Unit Selection

The wide array of problems identified in the RECON process permits researchers, funders, educators, counselors, and even target group members to discuss together the problems in a clearer, more focused, way. The SMQ, which provides norms and the frequency distribution of the problems in the population, adds to our sense of the relative importance of different problems.

Quite probably, there will not initially be enough funds to develop units for all of the problems thus, it will be necessary to select the most important problems for initial unit development. Generally, these are problems, the resolution of which, will help to resolve other secondary or tertiary problems or will facilitate the target group's ability to solve other problems by themselves.

We recommend that the RECON data, collected from urban black single mothers, be fused in a funding conference which includes all of the interested parties but, especially, the researchers, funders, and local program administrators, in determining which units are important enough to be developed first. The unit selection conference has the secondary value of helping to insure that all people involved in the eventual dissemination of the program have a common commitment.

Program Design

The strategy of program design involves planning for a four stage learning unit which specifies learning activities, media, and sequences.

In actual program design, having selected the learning tracks to be developed into learning units, the research team designs a Four Stage learning sequence consisting of the Stimulus Stage, the Evocation Stage, the Objective Inquiry Stage, and the Application

Stage. The Four Stage Learning Model was first noted in Chapter I. If the learning tracks, presented in Chapter IV, Tables 14 and 15, were to become actual learning units. a Four Stage Learning Sequence, fully describing the purpose and objectives of each stage would be prepared. Since the development of an illustrative learning unit is also beyond the scope of this study, the reader is directed to the best example of this process in its completion, the *Adkins Life Skills Program:Career Development Series* (Adkins, Manuele, Lovett, Davis, and Cullinane, 1985). Further information regarding the series can be obtained by contacting the Institute for Life Coping Skills (Appendix E).

Testout, Evaluation, and Revision

Once the learning unit is fully developed it should be tested in the protected setting of the research and development center by a Life Skills Educator. Following evaluation and revisions, the unit is tested again in a field setting, evaluated, and revised again.

Since, for this description of the Life Skills program development process, the assumption has already been made that funding and other resources are not an obstacle, ideally, there would be several research and development centers across the country, in urban and rural areas, working on parenting and personal development programs with black single mothers. Ideally, those centers would field test their learning units in numerous settings available to the target groups (e.g.,adult learning centers, community organizations, social services agencies, community colleges, etc.). After an extensive testout, evaluation, and revision process, selected learning units would be ready for publication.

Development of Materials

The development of media materials is the next step in the program development process and the step which usually involves the most effort, time, and money. Since the Life Skills Program Model is typically video-based, this step requires not only the development of print and audio materials but of video materials as well. Research and development staff would develop the print based materials and the manuals and experienced video producers would be hired by the development center to work with the design team on the production of scripts and relevant video sequences for the selected learning units.

Following that, actors and actresses would be hired to appear in the videos.

The design of the Four Stage Learning Unit for urban black single mothers would determine the kind and number of the video, print, and audio materials to be developed. Care would be taken to insure that they were culturally accurate and did in fact reflect the explicit problems and subtle nuances of the RECON.

Installation

Following publication, installation of a Life Skills program usually involves its introduction into an existing educational setting. The most important factor in installation is making sure that administrators and supervisors at the existing educational center understand the new program and its requirements so that they will be familiar with the necessary criteria for selecting Life Skills Educators (LSEs) and adjusting the schedules and rhythms of their institutions to make space for the program.

To assure access to the poorest of urban black single mothers, local community organizations such as churches, public schools, community mental health clinics, adult learning centers, libraries, daycare centers, etc., must be involved. Development centers and/or publishers would work closely with these organizations to plan the logistics involved in installing and conducting the program effectively.

Because the Life Skills model and the current Life Skills Educator Training Program (Adkins, Adkins, and Kessler, 1987) provides training of LSEs in Life Skills theory and concepts, program installation, teaching, and counseling, people who are not counselors by profession can be trained to deliver the program. It is foreseeable that some former program participants would eventually be trained as LSEs, and the best of those would become trainers of LSEs.

Dissemination

The last step in the process, designed to make the program widely available, on a mass scale, is dissemination. Mass scale dissemination follows the effective development of a marketing program throughout the country. Of course mass dissemination would require the funding and support of the government as well as the overall support of the public. Later in this Chapter, recommendations for building supportive environments for Life Skills Parent Education program development will be discussed

Other Related Activities

As the program is disseminated throughout the country, a series of other important and related activities, involved in facilitating the process, can be carried out by those involved in conducting on-site programs as well as by research and development center staff persons. Examples of these activities are; training of LSEs, revisions to the Life Skills Educators Training Program (LSETP), follow-up visits to program sites, and evaluations of program site effectiveness. In addition to these activities, research and development centers should take primary responsibility for the conducting of frequent professional conferences for LSEs so that they have opportunities to network and share information with each other about their programs.

CONCLUSIONS

This study concludes that urban black single mothers represent one parent group, among non-traditional families, that is sorely in need of additional supports and help in resolving psycho-social problems which impact upon them as persons and as parents. Although this need is especially true of poor urban black single mothers, it does not necessarily exclude non-poor mothers. The study also concludes that the creation of parenting and personal development programs, based on the Adkins Life Skills Model, offers one viable, practical, affordable, and potentially effective way of providing assistance to this parent group.

Why Should Help be Provided?

In the introduction to this study, articles, headlines, and statistics were cited which decried the increase in households headed by single mothers. Several factors were noted which raise cause for alarm. Among them are (1) higher infant mortality rates and other health risks due to poor or non-existent prenatal care for mothers and infants, (2) the fact that most single mothers tend to be poor and undereducated, (3) more and more teenagers are becoming single mothers and, (4) that mothers and children from economically deprived households are more likely to become involved with substance abuse and crime.

In addition, there is growing alarm in most of the inner cities of this country about the increasing welfare costs, the upward surge of homelessness, the deterioration of public education, the rise in AIDS cases, the proliferation of drug use and trafficking, and the increasing involvement of children and youth in gangs, drugs, and crime. In the inner cities, much of the focus of these concerns fall on black youth, who in many cases tend to come from the poorest and most disadvantaged homes. Homes which frequently are headed by single mothers.

As concerns grow, experts and interested citizens look for answers and places to lay blame. Although many places for blame have been found (e.g., peer pressure, welfarism, local and international drug pushers, gun manufacturers, underprepared and non-caring teachers, racism, the economic recession, Reaganism, etc.), few answers have been formulated. While few can deny the problems of today's troubled youth, many look only to sources outside of the family to resolve them.

In a newspaper article, Raspberry (1991), noting the collapse of the "nuclear" or traditional family, writes that "it makes sense to strengthen families as they exist." Raspberry concludes:

> It may be cheaper to teach families how to manage and nurture their children than to fund the clinics, the rehabilitation centers, and the foster-care system designed to rescue them after they've gone wrong (p. 49).

To say that a major part of the responsibility of raising children to be confident, well-behaved, and smart belongs with the family is not to say that factors such as economics, drugs, schools, etc., don't play a part. It does say, however, that there is little potential for success without parent involvement. Among other things, effective parenting involves using good judgment, making decisions, knowing about and using good child management skills. It also requires involvement in a child's life, on every level. The ability to parent well, however, is probably at least as much affected by poor ability to cope with personal issues and manage one's own life as by a lack of knowledge about specific child management skills. Both personal and parental learning is essential for helping parents be better parents.

Until now, there has neither been the national support nor the will, nor the community involvement to revise or create the policies that would help troubled families. However, polls now indicate that the American public has an overriding concern, not only with rising crime but, with the increasing numbers of children and youths involved in committing serious crimes.

In the closing section of this chapter, recommendations are made for changes that could support and strengthen all families, whether traditional or non-traditional, but with a special emphasis on families headed by poor urban black single mothers because, as this study has already established, this is a family group at high risk.

RECOMMENDATIONS FOR BUILDING SUPPORTIVE ENVIRONMENTS FOR AMERICAN FAMILIES

At many levels of government and society, policy changes are needed, which would establish the kinds of supportive environments in which all American families could thrive. Changes are needed which would not only make possible the creation and dissemination nationally of the type of parenting and personal development programs proposed by this study, but would provide the moral leadership and funding required to make the survival of our families a high priority.

Collaborative efforts in this regard, on the part of government and community can make a crucial difference in the lives of many families, particularly poor families.

As if to illustrate the need for change and collaboration in this regard, a New York Times (1991) article, deploring the entrenchment of urban poverty in American life, noted that an American anti-poverty policy is desperately needed and, that a want ad for such a social policy might list other requirements such as "a passionate leader to articulate it, taxpayers willing to pay for it, special interests that sacrifice for it, and skilled administrators to apply it." To critics who say that government programs for the poor do not work, the article goes on to quote advocates like Marian Wright Edelman of the Children's Defense Fund, who argue that there is ample evidence that government spending, if properly targeted on education, housing, health care, and job training can be invaluable in breaking the cycle of poverty. Certainly, the current plight of poor single mothers and children in this country only helps to emphasize the needs expressed in this article.

In addition to policy changes on the government level, changes need to take place in the business sector, in education, and in community thinking and involvement. These changes are needed to foster additional supports for urban black single mothers, as well as for other non-traditional parent groups, which would make more services and resources available to them generally and create environments in which these parents and their children have real opportunities to achieve to their full potentials.

Government Policy

National commitment to the American family. First, policy changes in support of families generally, and non-traditional families specifically, are required. There must be a new commitment to providing the time and dollars necessary to help poor and troubled families to change their lives. A strong national commitment to families would make possible the creation and widespread dissemination of parenting and personal development programs. As part of an intensive and comprehensive federally sponsored family survival program, the creation of this type of parent education offers a potentially effective modality for empowering, sustaining, and strengthening families on a mass scale in many cities across the country.

The federal government must give more than "lip service" to the crucial issue of parent development since the future of America depends on its youth. While in the past, the urgent needs of poor mothers and children may have been responded to by patching together makeshift and ineffective programs or, by attempting to "reinvent the wheel," in recent years, the federal government's response has been to neglect and ignore the issue almost entirely. It has done so, through its policies of cutbacks in critical social programs such as housing and health care. The disastrous results of this neglect, particularly on the poor, are clear to all of us as we look around at the thousands of homeless mothers of millions of homeless children. It seems obvious that the time has come for the federal government to take a leadership role in championing and supporting efforts to strengthen and preserve the American family, not just the traditional family (e.g., mother, father, and child) but, also the many non-traditional families that make up such a large portion of our population today.

Some recommendations for government intervention. The federal government should begin this process by fostering a national will and commitment to this cause. A committee on the preservation and strengthening of families should be established within the Department of Health, Education, and Welfare. Legislation should be enacted or changed to help states establish the type of program development centers advocated in this study in urban as well as other areas throughout the country. Sufficient funding and time commitments should be provided so that development centers can create quality programs without fearing the loss of dollars half way through their projects. The government should assist in the dissemination of completed programs on a mass scale so that an optimum number of mothers needing the programs can take advantage of them.

Government commitments of time and dollars. Time and funding commitments for a period of at least five years are necessary to carry out all of the program development steps described in this chapter. Considering the social problems faced today, due to long neglect, and, the problems we will face in the future if we continue to do so, five years seems a small amount of time to spend developing a tool with the potential of the parenting and personal development program.

Dollar commitments involve providing the necessary funds to create development centers, staff them, carry out the research and development work, test and evaluate the programs, revise the programs and, finally, disseminate the programs. Adkins, for example, with approximately a one-half million dollar grant, produced the *Adkins Life Skills Program:Employability Skills Series* (Adkins, Wylie, Grothe, Kessler, and Manuele, 1975). Today, that video based group counseling program, in its second edition, the *Career Development Series* (Adkins, et al., 1985), is used widely across the country by over 750 organizations, agencies, and schools in 42 states which are concerned with their clients' learning of career development and employability skills. Even at today's inflation rates, the costs of the proposed development effort seems minimal when measured against rising welfare and criminal justice costs and the many other costs associated with repairing the damage done to society by its neglect of the emotional and physical well-being of poor parents and children. If the federal government can spend nearly one billion dollars for one Stealth Bomber (The New York Times, 1991), it can surely find a minimal 100 million dollars for a parenting and personal development program that can potentially improve the lives of millions of American children and parents.

Moral leadership. By adopting policies which sustain and strengthen families and support life affirming home environments, the federal government will be providing the moral leadership required to establish a national will.

Results of national polls taken in many cities suggest that Americans, although generally aware of poor or homeless people, feel largely isolated from the problems of the poor (Applebome, 1991). In New York City, most people actually see and encounter the poor daily as they travel back and forth to work but generally say they feel lost when it comes to doing anything meaningful to help. Indications suggest that Americans might be more responsive to the poor if educated about the needs and, more importantly, are given guidance as to what someone specifically could do to make a difference. They need to be offered a variety of meaningful, helping activities from which they can select what they are reasonably able to do.

By focusing the nation's attention on the plight of many families headed by single women, the federal government can capture the attention of the American public and focus the very human instinct to help others on this parent group specifically and on poverty generally.

Other government supports. As it provides the essential moral leadership, the federal government can also do the following:

(1) Support the development of parent education programs for other parent groups as well as urban black single mothers (e.g., single fathers, teen parents, middle-class parents, etc.). The program models should take into account the differences in family structure, life experiences, and socioeconomic levels. By supporting parent education for all parents, the government will serve as a role model in helping society to change any negative views it holds about the single parent family (particularly that of the black single mother) as inherently dysfunctional and beyond repair.

(2) Support and put into effect, changes in the areas of taxation, health care provision, the workplace, and other institutions which enhance the ability of all families to function optimally.

(3) Offer incentives to states and municipalities as well as to private entities which encourage housing development for poor, low and middle income families.

(4) Support reforms in daycare legislation so that quality and affordable child care can be available to working and non-working mothers. To the latter, so that they have an opportunity to prepare themselves for work and self-sufficiency.

(5) Improve the public education system by identifying, promoting, and supporting the replication of effective education program models in poor urban areas. For example, programs like the School Development Program, founded by Dr. James Comer in New Haven, Connecticut, which has reportedly raised the academic performance of poor children by using teachers and social workers to get parents involved in the schools (DeParle and Applebome, 1991). Other effective education models for urban areas might also advocate smaller schools and smaller classes.

Community Involvement

Community commitment to the American family. Hopefully, with the spur of national leadership, state and local governments will also receive the impetus to take fuller responsibility for the strengthening of single parent families, resulting in greater community involvement. Again, it is important to re-emphasize that the creation and dissemination of the type of parent education proposed by this study, requires, in addition to government support, the support of public and private educational institutions, the business sector, human services agencies, neighborhood self-help groups, grassroots organizations, and churches. As an investment in their individual and collective futures, communities cannot afford to do less than government since they suffer most immediately and acutely when their families deteriorate. Long before the effects of this deterioration is recognized or felt on a national level, local communities feel and see its effects within their boundaries; in increased drug use, lowered property values, the flight of the middle class, higher crime rates, failing schools with rising drop-out rates, increased disease risks, higher birth rates among teens, and climbing infant mortality rates. Nationwide, neighborhoods and communities suffering from these problems do not need further deterioration to know that something must be done, but they may need help and leadership in deciding on what to do and how.

Recommendations for community intervention. Currently, there appears to be an appalling lack of leadership in regard to these essential human issues both on the national and local levels. Locally, however, there is a real opportunity for talented people, who really want change, and for people who have a community platform, to band together and begin to make things happen. The following recommendations represent some hypothetical examples of how a concerned public might organize in local communities to create supportive neighborhood environments for families.

Adopt-A-Family. Typically, in most disadvantaged urban centers, there are many churches. Ministers and pastors of local churches might begin an "Adopt-A-Family" (National Urban League, Inc., 1985) movement by organizing themselves and agreeing to work cooperatively to improve the lives of all poor and troubled families within their communities, but with a particular focus on poor, female headed families. Ministers seem the most likely, natural choices to lead this type of grassroots, neighborhood movement, since the very nature of their calling and purpose, and that of their institutions, is the relief of human suffering and the promotion of life-affirming environments.

Once organized, these concerned ministers can agree to involve their congregations collectively in outreach efforts to families in need. They can establish movements within movements, wherein several members of a congregation (an adopting group) could act as a support network for one single mother and her child/children. Each adopting group, after meeting and developing a plan, might canvass assigned areas of the community to find families who need and want help. After explaining the purpose of the movement to a family, the family would be encouraged to participate. In a cooperative effort between active churches, perhaps one Sunday per month could be devoted to this type of outreach activity.

Once families are recruited, the adopting groups could serve them in several ways. For example, they could counsel and help families to network with needed services and resources in the community. They could monitor families' access to health care, good nutrition, and other staples of life. They could provide emotional comfort and support on a day-to-day basis to families and refer them to professional help if serious problems are apparent. They could advocate for families and get outside help in landlord disputes, welfare mishaps or other legal difficulties. They could serve as mentors to mothers and as role models to children. Some of the adopting group members could provide child care services at times; perhaps providing safe havens after school, where "latchkey" children could stay, have a snack, and do their homework until their mothers arrived home. Finally, assuming that the type of parenting and personal development program, proposed in this study, is now widely available in urban areas (with many of the programs run on-site in churches and other facilities in the community), they could assure that each adopted single mother has an opportunity to participate in the parenting program.

If ministers, in communities like Central Harlem would take responsibility for working together to lead movements like "Adopt-A-Family," a great deal could be accomplished that would be effective in providing the kind of consistent, long-term, and meaningful help to urban black single mothers and their children that is needed. A real "Adopt-A-Family" effort, on the part of a community, involves doing everything that is possible to empower the families helped toward the ultimate goal of self-sufficiency. Each time that goal is reached, there are new contributing members of the community who can then reach out to help others in need.

Other community supports. At the same time that ministers are leading neighborhood residents in the outreach efforts to single parent families described above, they and other members of the community can actively petition local politicians' support and advocacy in accomplishing some of the policy and social changes recommended below that in the future will benefit all families:

(1) Colleges and graduate schools can be helped to recognize the importance of parent education as a field of study and encouraged to develop training programs and departments providing professional education and degrees in the field (e.g., program design and development and the teaching of parenting, etc.).

(2) Public and private high school curricula can be revised to include required courses in parenting.

(3) Neighborhood public schools can be encouraged to serve after hours and on weekends as community centers, opening their doors to neighborhood children, parents, and the elderly and providing recreation and tutorial services and rooms for community meetings.

(4) Businesses and corporations can be encouraged to provide on-site daycare or nursery facilities for working mothers of young children.

(5) Businesses and corporations can be encouraged to provide more flexible work schedules so that all working mothers can work and still fulfill their parenting roles.

(6) Public and private organizations and businesses within the community (e.g., mental health clinics, political clubs, restaurants,

health care facilities, etc.) can be encouraged to provide free services and resources to families in the community. For example, mental health and health care facilities, which are typically reimbursed by Medicaid for their services, can sponsor monthly fairs where discussions regarding specific children or women's health care issues take place and information is distributed. Local restaurants, instead of throwing away unused, day old, food supplies might have that food picked up and distributed daily to families in need.

Clearly, the recommendations made above in regard to government and community support of families are not meant to be an exhaustive list, but rather, ideas that might generate more ideas in this area. It is important to reiterate that any efforts on federal, state, or local government levels to help families must be assisted and supported by the efforts of the people in the neighborhoods and the wider communities in which all families live.

Community Support of Program Development

Establishing community program development centers. Finally, the following recommendations are intended as guidelines for communities to facilitate the actual establishment and start-up of program development centers dedicated to the creation of parenting and personal development programs. The recommendations assume the implementation of a national commitment to parent education in terms of funding, time, and moral leadership discussed above. These recommendations also assume that a system and structure has already been established for federal, state, and local governments to collaborate with involved persons and for all to be accountable in these efforts.

Funders and concerned community leaders representing business, education, and the clergy as well as program administrators and interested parents need to meet in urban areas across the country to discuss and formulate plans for the development of programs in their geographic regions. One result of these meetings, could be the formation of community councils with mandates to do the following during the program development phase:

(1) Acquire commitments from churches, schools, colleges, or other agencies within the community to cooperate in providing space for the establishment of program development and research centers as well as testout and evaluation environments.

(2) Seek the cooperation of involved organizations in staffing the centers, both with professionals (program designers and developers) and lay people. The centers should have members of the target population working there and have multi-racial staffs and advisory boards to symbolize and reflect the fact that the survival of the black family is not just a black person's problem nor responsibility.

(3) Involving single mothers appropriately in program development. For example, some will help to recruit other mothers, some will be RECON interview participants, some will be involved in test and evaluation groups, etc.

(4) Assist in coordinating the publication and dissemination of thoroughly tested, quality, proven effective parenting and personal development programs, on a mass scale, to serve the needs of targeted single parent populations across the country.

(5) When programs have been fully developed, involve a wide variety of community organizations at all levels in reaching out to single mothers within the community to identify those interested and, in need of, a parenting and personal development program.

In closing, this study has assessed the Life Skills learning needs of urban black single mothers as parents and as persons and has used the identified needs to create Preliminary Learning Tracks and Objectives for a Life Skills Parenting and Personal Development Program for Urban Black Single Mothers. The proposed program development, if financed by government and fully supported by the general public, the business sector, the educational community, the religious establishment, and dozens of other private and public agencies and organizations as previously described, offers hope that in the future proper values, emphasis, priorities, and resources will be allotted to the important role of parenting in our society. Once accomplished, not only families headed by women, but all families will benefit with improved emotional, physical, and economic functioning. The ultimate benefit will come to all of us when generations of poverty cycles are broken. The results will be an expanded national economy with millions of additional contributing taxpayers for generations to come, superior school systems, more jobs, and a better educated workforce to fill them, fewer homeless and a workable plan for helping those who are, improved health care systems, lowered crime statistics, thriving urban, suburban, and rural communities and, perhaps, better race relationships.

The promise is great but there is much to be done to improve the life chances of millions of parents and children. The type of parenting and personal development program development proposed in this study offers only one crucial step in the right direction.

APPENDIX A

Table A.1

Clinician Responses[a] to Problem Statements of RECON Participants

1. Problem Statement : My children don't share anything with me.

Clinician Response: This mother may be over-identifying with children. She should look at her own development. It's natural, to a degree, for children, especially adolescents, not to share their thoughts with a parent or any adult. Peers are confidants. Parents also have to learn to use their own experiences to open communication with a child.

2. Problem Statement : I don't have much of a social life.

Clinician Response: Evaluate the reasons why. Is it because you do not have anyone to babysit for you so that you can get out more? If so, try networking and sharing babysitting responsibilities with other mothers with similar needs. Is it because you don't have opportunities to meet people? Tell friends and relatives this is what you want. Take advantage of every chance to go out. Get involved with community, church, school and other activities. If there is a desire for male companionship, try not to let this need keep you from other social experiences. You might always meet a really great guy, maybe a single father, at the next PTA meeting. If working, take part in activities like bowling leagues with co-workers. If all fails, maybe you might need to evaluate whether this is what you really want or, whether it's what you think you should want. Counseling can help with this.

3. Problem Statement: It's difficult making them (children) understand that they can't have everything they see their friends have.

Clinician Response: Mother has to help the child see that he or she is not defined by the expense of, or number of, things owned. To do this, the parent has to believe it. She has to be a whole person herself. If so, she won't experience guilt because she takes this stand. Feeling deprived is a state of mind. Even if the mother has the money, she should not buy everything a child wants, simply because his or her friends have it.

4. Problem Statement: I need to learn to budget my money better.

Clinician Response: This mother needs to sit down, take a pencil and paper and begin to take a look at where her money is going. Keep a record for at least one month of where every dime goes. Of course she should include bills like utilities, food and so forth, but don't forget to write down unplanned spending. Even small amounts add up. A nickel here and a dime there for candy or the like can soon become quite a monthly expense with children. Carry a small pad with a pencil in her bag and try to jot down every expenditure. After keeping this record for awhile, she'll have a clearer picure of where her money goes and, of where she needs to cut back. After this exploratory period, startto develop a real budget. Set aside what's needed on a weekly basis for necessities, savings (if she can afford any) and recreation. Do not, and I cannot emphasize it enough, DO NOT be discouraged because there is not much for the latter two after dealing with necessities. Just as you can be nickled and dimed into bankruptcy, so you can nickel and dime your way to a bank savings account and/or an occasional family outing. Teach children to budget and save at every opportunity.

5. Problem Statement: I haven't talked with my thirteen year old son about sex but I know that he is interested. (Note: Mother found copies of nude magazines in son's room).

Clinician Response: She should make time for discussing child's natural interests in sex and use it as an opportunity to teach. Newspaper articles can be used as openers. Explore nature of child's involvement with someone. Know what is overstimulating for youngster. Set rules.

6. Problem Statement: There are just not enough hours in the day to get everything done. I'm just exhausted.

Clinician Response: This statement could mean a number of things or signal a number of needs. If it is an organizational or time management problem, planning ahead helps. For example, planning the dinner menu a week in advance helps. On weekends, if mother works, she should attempt to cook at least two or three meals which can be heated up during the week. Also, shopping for the week means the necessary ingredients are in the house for planned meals. Children who are old enough should be involved in helping, either assisting with or preparing meals and in cleaning up afterwards. A weekly schedule for mother and children, posted in the kitchen, is usually quite good. It reminds people of where they are suppose to be, when, and what they are suppose to be doing. Although better organizational skills may be needed, sometimes this complaint masks other problems, like depression. Frequently, when overwhelmed, a mother may be unable to function up to her normal capability due to stress, agitation or tension. She may express this as tiredness, irritability, or physical illness. If depression is the problem, she will not be able to benefit from learning better time management techniques or organizational skills until the depression is dealt with. In such a case, a professional referral for mental health services may be needed.

7. <u>Problem Statement:</u> I have problems getting my children do do household chores.

<u>Clinician Response:</u> It is difficult, once children reach a certain age and have not been taught to feel responsible for helping out at home. Begin very early, even when they are toddlers, to teach children to take responsibility at home. Start by letting toddlers help you to put away toys after play. As children get older, add other chores that are within their abilities to do developmentally. While children are young, it's so easy to make a game of sweeping, dusting, making beds and such. At the same time, it's an opportunity to teach and let the child feel grown-up. To prevent sibling bickering, specific chores should be assigned to specific children. When assigned chores are not done, punish by withholding or restricting things the child enjoys like TV, movies, etc. Allowances should not be tied in to every household chore if a sense of family responsibility is to be developed.

8. <u>Problem Statement:</u> There is no place to take children that you don't have to spend money.

<u>Clinician Response:</u> Sometimes parents need to stop defining recreational or leisure time with children in terms of how much it costs. Quality time does not have to be costly time. It is not necessary to always take children someplace to have a good time. Everyday

activities can be turned into pleasurable teaching/learning experiences for the family. For example, everyone has to shop for necessities. Even the usually tiring food shopping trip can be fun. Talk to children while shopping. Teach them things they need to know about consumerism. Mother needs to know that sometimes her child may be quite content to have her company and attention, even if they just stay home and play a game or watch TV together. As for places to go that do not cost money, how about a picnic in a nearby park or, on the living room floor in the winter? Make tuna fish or peanut butter sandwiches or fried chicken for the picnic. Don't buy fast foods, it's too expensive and encourages children to eat junk food. Plan the activity, whatever it is, with the children and do not attempt to hide money limitations. Start early, everything depends on what kids are raised to expect.

---

[a] Clinician responses are not exact quotes.

APPENDIX B

Table B.1

SMQ III - Problem Statements Rated as Belonging to the Parenting Category by Item Number

Item Numbers[a]
2, 3, 4, 5, 6, 7, 8, 9, 10, 11, 12, 13, 14, 15, 16, 17, 18, 20, 23, 24, 25, 26, 27, 28, 29, 30, 32, 33, 34, 36, 37, 39, 40, 42, 43, 44, 45, 47, 48, 50, 52, 53, 54, 56, 57, 58, 59, 60, 62, 63, 64, 66, 67, 68, 69, 70, 71, 73, 74, 76, 77, 78, 79, 80, 81, 82, 84, 86, 88

Table B.2

SMQ III - Problem Statements Rated as Belonging to the Personal Growth and Development Category by Item Number

Item Numbers
1, 19, 21, 22, 27, 31, 35, 38, 41, 46, 49, 50, 51, 55, 61, 65, 72, 75, 80, 83, 85, 86, 87, 89, 90

[a] Items 27, 50, 80, and 86 are included in both categories.

APPENDIX C

Single Mother Questionnaire

PART I

Instructions: This group of questions is designed to get background information on respondents. Please answer each question.

1. What is your age? ________ Race? ________________

2. Were you born in the U.S.? Yes _______ No ___________

3. If not born in the U.S. where were you born?_________________

4. If not born in the U.S. how many years have you lived here?_______

5. Where do you live now?
City/town ______________________________________
Borough or neighborhood (Harlem, Bedford Stuyvesant, etc.)
____

6. How long have you lived in your present neighborhood? (In years)
____

7. How many children do you have? _________________________

8. Number of boys ______ Ages ________________________

9. Number of girls ______ Ages ________________________

10. How many children live with you? _________________________

11. Are you: (Please check one)
Divorced ___________ How long? ____________
Widowed ___________ How long? ____________
Separated ___________ How long? ____________
Never Married _______

12. Are you employed? Yes _______ No ____________

13. If employed, what type of work do you do? ____________________

____

14. If employed, are you satisfied with your job? Yes ___ No _____

15. If dissatisfied with your job, why? ____________________________

____

16. What type of work would you like to do? ______________________

____

17. Please check your annual income bracket (include all sources of income)

    ___________ Under $5,000
    ___________ $6,000 to $10,000
    ___________ $11,000 to $15,000
    ___________ $16,000 to $20,000
    ___________ over $20,000

18. Are you receiving income from any of the sources below? (Please check all from which you receive income).

    ___________ child support/alimony
    ___________ welfare
    ___________ social security
    ___________ job
    ___________ other (please specify) _______________________

19. Is your annual income enough to support you and your children?

20. To what religion do you belong?

    _____ Methodist
    _____ Baptist
    _____ Catholic
    _____ Lutheran
    _____ Other (please specify) _____________________________
    _____ None

21. Do you consider yourself a religious person? Yes ____No ____

22. Last school grade completed ___________________________________

23. Are you interested in returning to school? Yes ____No ____

24. If yes, what do you want to study? ____________________________

Single Mother Questionnaire

Part II

Instructions: This part of the questionnaire is designed to look at how easy it is for you to get help. Please answer each question.

1. Do you have someone you can depend on when there is an unexpected problem with your children? Yes _____ No ______

2. Is this person a:
   _______ Relative
   _______ Friend
   _______ Neighbor
   _______ Other (please specify) ________________________________

3. Does your mother help you on a regular basis with childcare?
   Yes __________ No __________

4. If your mother does not help you, why?
   _______ Lives too far away
   _______ Works
   _______ Has other children to care for
   _______ Deceased
   _______ Other (please specify) ________________________________

5. Does anyone else help you on a regular basis? Yes ___ No ___
   If yes, who? (e.g., friend, relative, etc.) __________________________

6. Have you tried to get counseling to help with personal problems from a counselor, minister, or other professional within the past year for:
   _______ Yourself
   _______ One or more of your children
   _______ You and one or more of your children
   _______ No

7. Were you able to get counseling to help with personal problems from a counselor, minister or other professional within the past year for:
   _______ Yourself
   _______ One or more of your children
   _______ Yourself and one or more of your children
   _______ No

8. Do you feel some type of counseling might be helpful now for:

_______ Yourself
_______ One or more of your children
_______ Yourself and one or more of your children
_______ No

Single Mother Questionnaire

Part III

The following portion of the questionnaire is intended to identify some areas that concern single mothers living in large cities.

Each statement will be followed by the responses STRONGLY AGREE - AGREE - DISAGREE - STRONGLY DISAGREE. For each statement, please circle the response that best expresses your feeling about the statement. Please be sure to answer each statement by circling only ONE response.

---

1. I feel I never have enough time for myself.

STRONGLY AGREE AGREE DISAGREE STRONGLY DISAGREE

2. Children need to have rules to follow.

STRONGLY AGREE AGREE DISAGREE STRONGLY DISAGREE

3. I think that teenage children are difficult to talk to.

STRONGLY AGREE AGREE DISAGREE STRONGLY DISAGREE

4. My children need a man in their lives on a regular basis.

STRONGLY AGREE AGREE DISAGREE STRONGLY DISAGREE

5. I worry about the time my children spend alone while I'm working or out of the house for other reasons.

STRONGLY AGREE AGREE DISAGREE STRONGLY DISAGREE

6. I have problems making my children obey rules.

STRONGLY AGREE AGREE DISAGREE STRONGLY DISAGREE

7. I feel I never have enough time for my children.

STRONGLY AGREE AGREE DISAGREE STRONGLY DISAGREE

8. I can usually count on getting help from family and friends.

STRONGLY AGREE AGREE DISAGREE STRONGLY DISAGREE

9. Trying to think of ways to entertain my children is very hard.

STRONGLY AGREE AGREE DISAGREE STRONGLY DISAGREE

10. There is never enough money to go places or buy things for children.

STRONGLY AGREE AGREE DISAGREE STRONGLY DISAGREE

11. I think mothers especially need a man to make boys obey.

STRONGLY AGREE AGREE DISAGREE STRONGLY DISAGREE

12. I sometimes feel guilty about my children not being with their father.

STRONGLY AGREE AGREE DISAGREE STRONGLY DISAGREE

13. I worry about drugs and other street crime in my community affecting my children.

STRONGLY AGREE AGREE DISAGREE STRONGLY DISAGREE

14. Public schools do a good job of educating children.

STRONGLY AGREE AGREE DISAGREE STRONGLY DISAGREE

15. My children sometimes tattle or lie on each other.

STRONGLY AGREE AGREE DISAGREE STRONGLY DISAGREE

16. I can be both mother and father to my children.

STRONGLY AGREE AGREE DISAGREE STRONGLY DISAGREE

17. I don't like many of my children's friends.

STRONGLY AGREE AGREE DISAGREE STRONGLY DISAGREE

18. I have to yell to get the children to do what I want.

STRONGLY AGREE AGREE DISAGREE STRONGLY DISAGREE

19. Support groups for single mothers is a good idea.

STRONGLY AGREE AGREE DISAGREE STRONGLY DISAGREE

20. Children need to be seen and not heard.

STRONGLY AGREE AGREE DISAGREE STRONGLY DISAGREE

21. I know what I want to do regarding my career and/or education.

STRONGLY AGREE AGREE DISAGREE STRONGLY DISAGREE

22. I don't have much of a social life.

STRONGLY AGREE AGREE DISAGREE STRONGLY DISAGREE

23. Children need to be taught about sex and their own sexual development.

STRONGLY AGREE AGREE DISAGREE STRONGLY DISAGREE

24. If my children failed a subject in school I would punish them.

STRONGLY AGREE AGREE DISAGREE STRONGLY DISAGREE

25. It's natural for brothers and sisters to be jealous of each other.

STRONGLY AGREE AGREE DISAGREE STRONGLY DISAGREE

26. The best way to handle questions about sex from little children is to ignore them.

STRONGLY AGREE AGREE DISAGREE STRONGLY DISAGREE

27. I often feel overburdened with the responsibilities of being a single parent.

STRONGLY AGREE AGREE DISAGREE STRONGLY DISAGREE

28. Finding dependable childcare that I can afford is almost impossible.

STRONGLY AGREE AGREE DISAGREE STRONGLY DISAGREE

29. I find it hard to make my children understand that they can't have everything they want.

STRONGLY AGREE AGREE DISAGREE STRONGLY DISAGREE

30. There's really no place to take children where you don't have to spend money.

STRONGLY AGREE AGREE DISAGREE STRONGLY DISAGREE

31. I feel exhausted most of the time.

STRONGLY AGREE AGREE DISAGREE STRONGLY DISAGREE

32. Boys need a man to take them to baseball or basketball games.

STRONGLY AGREE AGREE DISAGREE STRONGLY DISAGREE

33. Too many young people in my neighborhood hang around in the streets.

STRONGLY AGREE AGREE DISAGREE STRONGLY DISAGREE

34. I think my children blame me or will blame me because their father is not living with us.

STRONGLY AGREE AGREE DISAGREE STRONGLY DISAGREE

35. People don't care about each other in the city.

STRONGLY AGREE AGREE DISAGREE STRONGLY DISAGREE

36. I think my children are overattached to me.

STRONGLY AGREE AGREE DISAGREE STRONGLY DISAGREE

37. I wish my children's father was more involved in their lives.

STRONGLY AGREE AGREE DISAGREE STRONGLY DISAGREE

38. I feel unsafe in my neighborhood.

STRONGLY AGREE AGREE DISAGREE STRONGLY DISAGREE

39. I don't think it's good to talk to my children about their father.

STRONGLY AGREE AGREE DISAGREE STRONGLY DISAGREE

40. Children raised in two-parent homes are better off emotionally.

STRONGLY AGREE AGREE DISAGREE STRONGLY DISAGREE

41. When I spend money or time on myself I feel selfish.

STRONGLY AGREE AGREE DISAGREE STRONGLY DISAGREE

42. I wish my children's father was less involved in their lives.

STRONGLY AGREE AGREE DISAGREE STRONGLY DISAGREE

43. My children know what I expect of them.

STRONGLY AGREE AGREE DISAGREE STRONGLY DISAGREE

44. Children raised in two-parent homes are better off financially.

STRONGLY AGREE AGREE DISAGREE STRONGLY DISAGREE

45. Boys need to learn to cook and clean just like girls.

STRONGLY AGREE AGREE DISAGREE STRONGLY DISAGREE

46. I would like to know about any clubs or activities for single parents in my community.

STRONGLY AGREE AGREE DISAGREE STRONGLY DISAGREE

47. I think my children are too passive.

STRONGLY AGREE AGREE DISAGREE STRONGLY DISAGREE

48. I often lose patience with my children.

STRONGLY AGREE AGREE DISAGREE STRONGLY DISAGREE

49. I would like to spend more time with adult company than I do now.

STRONGLY AGREE AGREE DISAGREE STRONGLY DISAGREE

50. I wish I had someone to help me with the job of parenting.

STRONGLY AGREE AGREE DISAGREE STRONGLY DISAGREE

51. I frequently find myself getting angry.

STRONGLY AGREE AGREE DISAGREE STRONGLY DISAGREE

52. There is nothing I can do to make the schools do a better job for my children.

STRONGLY AGREE AGREE DISAGREE STRONGLY DISAGREE

53. It's impossible to get my children to do household chores.

STRONGLY AGREE AGREE DISAGREE STRONGLY DISAGREE

54. My children need to learn how to study.

STRONGLY AGREE AGREE DISAGREE STRONGLY DISAGREE

55. I could use help in learning to budget my money better.

STRONGLY AGREE AGREE DISAGREE STRONGLY DISAGREE

56. Public schools do a good job of disciplining children.

STRONGLY AGREE AGREE DISAGREE STRONGLY DISAGREE

57. My children select what they want to see on TV.

STRONGLY AGREE AGREE DISAGREE STRONGLY DISAGREE

58. My children talk too much.

STRONGLY AGREE AGREE DISAGREE STRONGLY DISAGREE

59. If my children started having problems of any kind I know of someplace in my community where we could get help.

STRONGLY AGREE AGREE DISAGREE STRONGLY DISAGREE

60. I think it's okay if my children read comic books.

STRONGLY AGREE AGREE DISAGREE STRONGLY DISAGREE

61. I often feel lonely.

STRONGLY AGREE AGREE DISAGREE STRONGLY DISAGREE

62. Talking to young children about sex abuse will just scare them unnecessarily.

STRONGLY AGREE AGREE DISAGREE STRONGLY DISAGREE

63. The more things I but for my children, the less the appreciate it.

STRONGLY AGREE AGREE DISAGREE STRONGLY DISAGREE

64. You can't expect teenage children to talk much to their parents.

STRONGLY AGREE AGREE DISAGREE STRONGLY DISAGREE

65. I can't consider continuing my education now because I can't afford it.

STRONGLY AGREE AGREE DISAGREE STRONGLY DISAGREE

66. My children can watch TV and do their homework at the same time.

STRONGLY AGREE AGREE DISAGREE STRONGLY DISAGREE

67. Children mainly learn about sex in the streets.

STRONGLY AGREE AGREE DISAGREE STRONGLY DISAGREE

68. I expect my children to have homework every night.

STRONGLY AGREE AGREE DISAGREE STRONGLY DISAGREE

69. I think sex education belongs only in the home.

STRONGLY AGREE AGREE DISAGREE STRONGLY DISAGREE

70. When you have more than one child you can't give any one special attention.

STRONGLY AGREE AGREE DISAGREE STRONGLY DISAGREE

71. I believe in talking to my children about my feelings and beliefs.

STRONGLY AGREE AGREE DISAGREE STRONGLY DISAGREE

72. I think I'm too old to think about going back to school.

STRONGLY AGREE AGREE DISAGREE STRONGLY DISAGREE

73. There's not much I can do in my neighborhood to protect my children from the dangers of the street.

STRONGLY AGREE AGREE DISAGREE STRONGLY DISAGREE

74. When my children fail in school I know it's because they are lazy.

STRONGLY AGREE AGREE DISAGREE STRONGLY DISAGREE

75. I believe that people's experiences with public agencies like welfare, social security, or unemployment are usually unpleasant.

STRONGLY AGREE AGREE DISAGREE STRONGLY DISAGREE

76. I can't expect my children to earn money while they are going to school.

STRONGLY AGREE AGREE DISAGREE STRONGLY DISAGREE

77. It's natural for a young child to be jealous of a new baby.

STRONGLY AGREE AGREE DISAGREE STRONGLY DISAGREE

78. I think birth control information should be given to children.

STRONGLY AGREE AGREE DISAGREE STRONGLY DISAGREE

79. My children have to earn allowances.

STRONGLY AGREE AGREE DISAGREE STRONGLY DISAGREE

80. I believe that a good education is the key to success.

STRONGLY AGREE AGREE DISAGREE STRONGLY DISAGREE

81. I find many things my children talk about interesting.

STRONGLY AGREE AGREE DISAGREE STRONGLY DISAGREE

82. I don't believe I can spoil my children by giving them the things their friends have.

STRONGLY AGREE AGREE DISAGREE STRONGLY DISAGREE

83. I can't consider continuing my education now because I have no time.

STRONGLY AGREE AGREE DISAGREE STRONGLY DISAGREE

84. I trust my children.

STRONGLY AGREE AGREE DISAGREE STRONGLY DISAGREE

85. Racial discrimination has not affected my life.

STRONGLY AGREE AGREE DISAGREE STRONGLY DISAGREE

86. The best thing for me and my children would be to move from our present community.

STRONGLY AGREE AGREE DISAGREE STRONGLY DISAGREE

87. I think that a woman should be able to have an abortion if she wants one.

STRONGLY AGREE AGREE DISAGREE STRONGLY DISAGREE

88. Its more important for girls to spend time with their mothers than with their fathers.

STRONGLY AGREE AGREE DISAGREE STRONGLY DISAGREE

89. I think that I am an attractive person.

STRONGLY AGREE AGREE DISAGREE STRONGLY DISAGREE

90. I sometimes feel discriminated against because I'm a woman.

STRONGLY AGREE AGREE DISAGREE STRONGLY DISAGREE

APPENDIX D

Table D.1

Significant Problem Statements of the SMQ, Part III (N = 55)

Learning Category: PERSONAL GROWTH AND DEVELOPMENT

Problem Area	Item No.	Problem Statement	% of A or D[a]	S or N[b]
1. Managing Money	10	There is never enough money to go places or buy things the children need.	80 A	S
	28	Finding dependable child care that I can afford is almost impossible.	67 A	S
	29	I find it hard to make my children understand that they can't have everything they want.	58 A	S
	30	There's really no place to take children where you don't have to spend money.	75 A	S
	41	When I spend money or time on myself I feel selfish.	33 A	N
	44	Children raised in two-parent homes are better off financially.	69 A	S
	55	I could use help in learning to budget my money better.	64 A	S

[a] A = Agree, D = Disagree
[b] S = Significant, N = Not Significant

Significant Problem Statements of the SMQ, Part III (N = 55)

Learning Category: PERSONAL GROWTH AND DEVELOPMENT

Problem Area	Item No.	Problem Statement	% of A or D[a]	S or N[b]
	63	The more things I buy for my children, the less they appreciate it.	62 A	S
	65	I can't consider continuing my education now because I can't afford it.	55 A	S
	76	I can't expect my children to earn money while they are going to school.	53 D	S
	79	My children have to earn allowance.	87 A	S
2. Overcoming Lack of Support, Alienation and Loneliness	8	I can usually count on getting help from family or friends.	58 D	S
	19	Support groups for single mothers is a good idea.	96 A	S
	22	I don't have much of a social life.	67 A	S
	27	I often feel overburdened with the responsibilities of being a single parent.	71 A	S

[a] A = Agree, D = Disagree
[b] S = Significant, N = Not Significant

Significant Problem Statements of the SMQ, Part III (N = 55)

Learning Category: PERSONAL GROWTH AND DEVELOPMENT

Problem Area	Item No.	Problem Statement	% of A or D[a]	S or N[b]
	35	People don't care about each other in the city.	71 A	S
	37	I wish my children's father was more involved in their lives.	71 A	S
	38	I feel unsafe in my neighborhood.	31 A	N
	46	I would like to know about any clubs or activities for single parents in my community.	92 A	S
	49	I would like to spend more time with adult company than I do now.	70 A	S
	50	I wish I had someone to help me with the job of parenting.	73 A	S
	51	I frequently find myself getting angry.	64 A	S
	61	I often feel lonely.	51 A	S
	73	There's not much I can do in my neighborhood to protect my children from the dangers of the streets.	27 A	N

[a] A = Agree, D = Disagree
[b] S = Significant, N = Not Significant

Significant Problem Statements of the SMQ, Part III (N = 55)

Learning Category: PERSONAL GROWTH AND DEVELOPMENT

Problem Area	Item No.	Problem Statement	% of A or D[a]	S or N[b]
	75	I believe that people's experiences with public agencies like welfare, social security or unemployment are usually unpleasant.	82 A	S
	85	Racial discrimination has not affected my life.	62 D	S
	86	The best thing for me and my children would be to move from our present community.	54 A	S
	90	I sometimes feel I'm discriminated against because I'm a woman.	56 A	S
3. Handling Anger, Guilt Worry, and Frustration	1	I feel I never have enough time for myself.	82 A	S
	5	I worry about the time my children spend alone while I'm working or out of the house for other reasons.	85 A	S
	6	I have problems making my children obey rules.	55 A	S

[a] A = Agree, D = Disagree
[b] S = Significant, N = Not Significant

Significant Problem Statements of the SMQ, Part III (N = 55)

Learning Category: PERSONAL GROWTH AND DEVELOPMENT

Problem Area	Item No.	Problem Statement	% of A or D[a]	S or N[b]
	7	I feel I never have enough time for myself.	35 A	N
	10	There is never enough money to go places or buy things the children need.	80 A	S
	12	I sometimes feel guilty about my children not being with their father.	44 A	N
	13	I worry about drugs and other street crime in my community affecting my children.	91 A	S
	18	I have to yell to get the children to do what I want.	60 A	S
	22	I don't have much of a social life.	67 A	S
	27	I often feel overburdened with the responsibilities of being a single parent.	71 A	S

[a]A = Agree, D = Disagree
[b]S = Significant, N = Not Significant

Significant Problem Statements of the SMQ, Part III (N = 55)

Learning Category: PERSONAL GROWTH AND DEVELOPMENT

Problem Area	Item No.	Problem Statement	% of A or D[a]	S or N[b]
	28	Finding dependable child-care that I can afford is almost impossible.	67 A	S
	29	I find it hard to make my children understand that they can't have everything they want.	58 A	S
	31	I feel exhausted most of the time.	65 A	S
	33	Too many young people in my neighborhood hang around in the streets.	93 A	S
	34	I think my children blame me or will blame me because their father is not living with us.	25 A	N
	37	I wish my children's father was more involved in their lives.	71 A	S
	41	When I spend money or time on myself I feel selfish.	33 A	N
	48	I often lose patience with my children.	60 A	S

[a]A = Agree, D = Disagree
[b]S = Significant, N = Not Significant

Significant Problem Statements of the SMQ, Part III (N = 55)

Learning Category: PERSONAL GROWTH AND DEVELOPMENT

Problem Area	Item No.	Problem Statement	% of A or D[a]	S or N[b]
	49	I would like to spend more time with adult company than I do now.	70 A	S
	50	I wish I had someone to help me with the job of parenting.	73 A	S
	51	I frequently find myself getting angry.	64 A	S
	61	I often feel lonely.	51 A	S
	63	The more things I buy for my children, the less they appreciate it.	62 A	S
	65	I can't consider continuing my education now because I can't afford it.	55 A	S
	72	I think I'm too old to think about going back to school.	87 A	S
	83	I can't consider continuing education now because I have no time.	35 A	N
	85	Racial discrimination has not affected my life.	62 A	S

[a]A = Agree, D = Disagree
[b]S = Significant, N = Not Significant

Significant Problem Statements of the SMQ, Part III (N = 55)

Learning Category: PERSONAL GROWTH AND DEVELOPMENT

Problem Area	Item No.	Problem Statement	% of A or D[a]	S or N[b]
	86	The best thing for me and my children would be to move from our present community.	54 A	S
	90	I sometimes feel discriminated against because I'm a woman.	56 A	S
4. Managing Time	1	I feel I never have enough time for myself.	82 A	S
	5	I worry about the time my children spend alone while I'm working or out of the house for other reasons.	85 A	S
	7	I feel I never have enough time for my children.	35 A	N
	41	When I spend money or time on myself I feel selfish.	33 A	N
	49	I would like to spend more time with adult company than I do now.	70 A	S
	70	When you have more than one child you can't give any one special attention.	62 A	S

[a]A = Agree, D = Disagree
[b]S = Significant, N = Not Significant

Significant Problem Statements of the SMQ, Part III (N = 55)

Learning Category: PERSONAL GROWTH AND DEVELOPMENT

Problem Area	Item No.	Problem Statement	% of A or D[a]	S or N[b]
	83	I can't consider continuing my education now because I have no time.	35 A	N
5. Planning for Career and Education	21	I know what I want to do regarding my career and/ or education.	82 A	S
	65	I can't consider continuing my education now because I can't afford it.	55 A	S
	72	I think I'm too old to think about going back to school.	87 A	S
	80	I believe that a good education is the key to success.	93 A	S
	83	I can't consider continuing my education now because I have no time.	35 A	N

[a]A = Agree, D = Disagree
[b]S = Significant, N = Not Significant

Table D.2

Significant Problem Statements of the SMQ, Part III (N = 55)

Learning Category: PARENTING

Problem Area	Item No.	Problem Statement	% of A or D[a]	S or N[b]
1. Educating Children	14	Public schools do a good job of educating children.	56 D	S
	24	If my children failed a subject in school I would punish them.	31 A	N
	52	There is nothing I can do to make the schools do a better job for my children.	25 A	N
	54	My children need to learn how to study.	75 A	S
	56	Public schools do a good job of disciplining children.	93 D	S
	57	My children select what they want to see on TV.	64 A	S
	66	My children can watch TV and do their homework at the same time.	7 A	N
	68	I expect my children to have homework every night.	80 A	S

[a] A = Agree, D = Disagree
[b] S = Significant, N = Not Significant

Significant Problem Statements of the SMQ, Part III (N = 55)

Learning Category: PARENTING

Problem Area	Item No.	Problem Statement	% of A or D[a]	S or N[b]
	74	When my children fail in school I know it's because they are lazy.	40 A	N
	76	I can't expect my children to earn money while they are going to school.	53 D	S
2. Communicating with Children	3	I think that teenage children are difficult to talk to.	62 A	S
	20	Children need to be seen and not heard.	27 A	N
	23	Children need to be taught about sex and their own sexual development.	98 A	S
	26	The best way to handle questions about sex from little children is to ignore them.	4 A	N
	29	I find it hard to make my children understand that they can't have everything they want.	58 A	S

[a] A = Agree, D = Disagree
[b] S = Significant, N = Not Significant

Significant Problem Statements of the SMQ, Part III (N = 55)

Learning Category: PARENTING

Problem Area	Item No.	Problem Statement	% of A or D[a]	S or N[b]
	39	I don't think it's good to talk to my children about their father.	24 A	N
	43	My children know what I expect of them.	89 A	S
	58	My children talk too much.	45 A	N
	62	Talking to young children about sex abuse will just scare them unnecessarily.	15 A	N
	64	You can't expect teenage children to talk much to their parents.	38 A	N
	67	Children mainly learn about sex in the streets.	75 A	S
	69	I think sex education belongs only in the home.	25 A	N
	71	I believe in talking to my children about my feelings and beliefs.	98 A	S
	78	I think birth control information should be given to teenagers.	96 A	S

[a] A = Agree, D = Disagree
[b] S = Significant, N = Not Significant

Significant Problem Statements of the SMQ, Part III (N = 55)

Learning Category: PARENTING

Problem Area	Item No.	Problem Statement	% of A or D[a]	S or N[b]
	81	I find many things my children talk about interesting.	94 A	S
3. Protecting Children from Crime	5	I worry about the time my children spend alone while I'm working or out of the house for other reasons.	85 A	S
	13	I worry about drugs and other street crime in my community affecting my children.	91 A	S
	33	Too many young people in my neighborhood hang around in the streets.	93 A	S
	38	I feel unsafe in my neighbor-hood.	31 A	N
	73	There's not much I can do in my neighborhood to protect my children from the dangers of the streets.	27 A	N
	86	The best thing for me and my children would be to move from our present community.	54 A	S

[a] A = Agree, D = Disagree
[b] S = Significant, N = Not Significant

Significant Problem Statements of the SMQ, Part III (N = 55)

Learning Category: PARENTING

Problem Area	Item No.	Problem Statement	% of A or D[a]	S or N[b]
4. Disciplining Children	2	Children need to have rules to follow.	98 A	S
	6	I have problems making my children obey rules.	55 A	S
	11	I think mothers especially need a man to make boys obey.	47 A	S
	15	My children sometimes tattle or lie on each other.	67 A	S
	17	I don't like many of my children's friends.	29 A	N
	18	I have to yell to get the children to do what I want.	60 A	S
	24	If my children failed a subject in school I would punish them.	31 A	N
	25	It's natural for brothers and sisters to be jealous of each other.	60 A	S
	29	I find it hard to make my children understand that they can't have everything they want.	58 A	S

[a] A = Agree, D = Disagree
[b] S = Significant, N = Not Significant

Significant Problem Statements of the SMQ, Part III (N = 55)

Learning Category: PARENTING

Problem Area	Item No.	Problem Statement	% of A or D[a]	S or N[b]
	43	My children know what I expect of them.	89 A	S
	53	It's impossible to get my children to do household chores.	40 A	N
	54	My children need to learn how to study.	75 A	S
	56	Public schools do a good job of disciplining children.	93 D	S
	57	My children select what they want to see on TV.	64 A	S
	59	If my children started having problems of any kind, I know of someplace in my community where we could get help.	54 A	S
	60	I think it's OK if my children read comic books.	85 A	S
	63	The more things I buy for my children, the less they appreciate it.	62 A	S
	66	My children can watch TV and do their homework at the same time.	7 A	N

[a] A = Agree, D = Disagree
[b] S = Significant, N = Not Significant

Significant Problem Statements of the SMQ, Part III (N = 55)

Learning Category: PARENTING

Problem Area	Item No.	Problem Statement	% of A or D[a]	S or N[b]
	77	It's natural for a young child to be jealous of a new baby.	87 A	S
	79	My children have to earn allowances.	87 A	S
	82	I don't believe I can spoil my children by giving them the things their friends have.	60 D	S
	84	I trust my children.	88 A	S
5. Identifying Positive Role Models	4	My children need a man in their lives on a regular basis.	73 A	S
	11	I think mothers especially need a man to make boys obey.	47 A	N
	12	I sometimes feel guilty about my children not being with their father.	44 A	N
	16	I can be both mother and father to my children.	51 D	S
	32	Boys need a man to take them to baseball or basket-ball games.	44 A	N

[a] A = Agree, D = Disagree
[b] S = Significant, N = Not Significant

Significant Problem Statements of the SMQ, Part III (N = 55)

Learning Category: PARENTING

Problem Area	Item No.	Problem Statement	% of A or D[a]	S or N[b]
	34	I think my children blame me because their father is not living with us.	25 A	N
	36	I think my children are overattached to me.	56 A	S
	37	I wish my children's father was more involved in their lives.	71 A	S
	40	Children raised in two-parent homes are better off emotionally.	47 A	S
	42	I wish my children's father was less involved in their lives.	14 A	N
	44	Children raised in two-parent homes are better off financially.	69 A	S
	45	Boys need to learn to cook and clean just like girls.	100 A	S
	47	I think my children are too passive.	80 A	S
	50	I wish I had someone to help me with the job of parenting.	73 A	S

[a] A = Agree, D = Disagree
[b] S = Significant, N = Not Significant

Significant Problem Statements of the SMQ, Part III (N = 55)

Learning Category: PARENTING

Problem Area	Item No.	Problem Statement	% of A or D[a]	S or N[b]
	88	It's more important for girls to spend time with their mothers than with their fathers.	61 D	S
6. Finding Affordable Leisure Activities	5	I worry about the time my children spend alone while I'm working or out of the house for other reasons.	85 A	S
	7	I feel I never have enough time for my children.	35 A	N
	8	I can usually count on getting help from family or friends.	58 D	S
	9	Trying to think of ways to entertain my children is very hard.	67 A	S
	10	There is never enough money to go places or buy things the children need.	80 A	S
	30	There's really no place to take children where you don't have to spend money.	75 A	S

[a] A= Agree, D= Disagree
[b] S = Significant, N = Not Significant

APPENDIX E

The Institute for Life Coping Skills, Inc.
Teachers College, Columbia University
Box 138, 525 W. 120th Street
New York, New York 10027

(212) 678-3181

References

Adkins, W.R. (1970). Life Skills: Structured counseling for the disadvantaged. *Personnel and Guidance Journal, 49,* 108-116.

Adkins, W.R. (1973, June). Life skills education for adult learners. *Adult Leadership, 22,* 55-58, 82-84.

Adkins, W.R. (1974). Life coping skills: A fifth curriculum. *Teachers College Record. 25,* 509-526.

Adkins, W.R. (1984). Life skills education: A video-based counseling/learning delivery system. In D. Larson (Ed.), *Teaching Psychological Skills: Models for Giving Psychology Away.* Monterey: Brooks/Cole.

Adkins, W.R., Adkins, C.M. & Kessler, M.M. (1987). *Life Skills Educator Training Program Manual.* New York: Institute for Life Coping Skills, Inc.

Adkins, W.R., Hattauer, E.A., Kessler, M.M. & Manuele, C.A. (1977) Where they hurt: A study of the life coping problems of unemployed adults. Unpublished manuscript. Teachers College, Columbia University.

Adkins, W.R., Manuele, C.A., Lovett, A.B., Davis, D. & Cullinane, M.C. (1985). *Adkins Life Skills Program: Career Development Series.* New York: Institute for Life Coping Skills, Inc.

Adkins, W.R., Rosenburg, S. & Sharar, P. (1965). *Training resources for youth: A comprehensive operational plan for a demonstration research training center for disadvantaged youth.* New York: Training Resources for Youth.

Adkins, W.R., Wylie, P., Grothe, M., Kessler, M. & Manuele, C. (1975). *Adkins Life Skills Program: Employability Skills Series.* New York: Psychological Corporation.

Applebome, P. (1991, January 28). Although urban blight worsens, most people don't feel its impact. *The New York Times,* pp. 81-83.

Authier, K.J., Sherrets, S.D. & Tramontana, M.G. (1980, Spring). Methods and models of parent education. *Journal of Clinical Child Psychology,* 38-39.

Badger, E. (1981). Effects of parent education program on teenage mothers and their offspring. In K.G. Scott, T. Field and E. Robertson (Eds.). *Teenage Parents and Their Offspring.* New York: Gruen and Stratton.

Belle, D. (1979). Depression and low income female-headed families. *Families Today: A Research Sampler on Families and Children.* Science Monographs No. 1. National Institute of Mental Health, 323-345.

Bigner, J.J. (1979). *Parent-child Relations.* New York: Macmillan.

Bilge, B. & Kaufman, G. (1983). Children of divorce and one-parent families: Cross cultural perspectives. *Family Relations, 32,* (1), 59-71.

Brackhaus, B. (1984). Needs assessment in adult education: Its problems and prospects. *Adult Education Forum, 27,* 233-239.

Bridgman, R.D. (1930). Postwar progress in child welfare. *Annals of the American Academy of Political and Social Science, 151,* 32-45.

Bronfenbrenner, U. (1972). The roots of alienation. In U. Brofenbenner (Ed.). *Influence on Human Development.* Hindsdale, Il: Dryden.

Burgess, J. (1970). The single parent family: A social and sociological problem. *The Famly Coordinator, 19,* 137-144.

Byrd, R. (1991, June 14). Births by unwed moms at record. *Daily News,* 7.

Center for the Study of Social Policy. (1984, March). *Working Female-Headed Families in Poverty: Three Studies of Low-Income Families Affected by the AFDC Policy Changes of 1981.* Washington, D.C.

Childcare Switchboard/Single Parent Resource Center. (1977, October). *Report of the Activities of the Single Parent Resource Center, 1975-76.* San Francisco, CA.

Clark-Stewart, K.A. (1978). Popular primers for parents. *American Psychologist, 33,* 359-369.

Cordes, C. (1984, August). The rise of one-parent black families. *APA Monitor,* 16-18.

Croake, J.W. & Glover, K.E. (1977, April). A history and evaluation of parent education. *The Family Coordinator,* 151-158.

Cronbach, L.J. (1951). Coefficient alpha and the internal structure of tests. *Psychometrika, 16,* 297-333.

Cronin, M., Pomper, S. & Simpson, J.C. (1990, September 17). The decline of New York. *Time,* 36-40, 41-44.

Cullinane, M.C. (1985). The effects of the Adkins Life Skills Program on the career choice of community college students. *Doctoral Dissertation, Teachers College, Columbia University.*

Datta, L. (978). Fron-end analysis: Pegasus or shank's mare? *New Directions for Program Evaluation, 1,* 13-30.

Dembo, M.H., Switzer, M. & Lauritzen, P. (1985, Summer). An evaluation of group parent education: Behavioral, PET, and Adlerian programs. *Review of Educational Research, 55,* (2), 155-200.

DeParle, J. & Applebome, P. (1991, January 29). Ideas to help poor abound but a consensus is wanting. *The New York Times,* C1-C3.

Department of City Planning, Community Assistance Unit, New York City. (1985). *Statement of Community District Needs, Fiscal Year 1985, Manhattan.* Office of Management and Budget. New York City.

Dickie, J.R. & Gerber, S.C. (1980). Training in social competence: The effect on mothers, fathers and infants. *Child Development, 51,* 1248-1251.

Fisher, K. (1984, August). Poor lack more than money. *A.P.A. Monitor, 38.*

Flintall, V.L. (1983). The effects of a behavioral training program in child management for potentially child abusing parents. *Doctoral Dissertation, Teachers College, Columbia University.*

Forehand, R., Middlebrook, J., Rogers, T. & Steffe, M. (1983). Dropping out of parent training. *Behavior Research and Therapy, 21,* (6), 663-668.

Freudenthal, K. (1959). Problems of the one-parent family. *Social Work, 4,* 44-49.

Gary, R.B. (1983). Black women and their utilization experiences with public agencies (Doctoral dissertation, University of Pennsylvania). *Social Work Research Abstracts. 20,* 989.

Gelman, D., Springen, K., Brailsford, K. & Miller, M. (1988, March 7). Black and white in America. *Newsweek,* 18-23.

Gorum, J.W. (1984). Stress-coping patterns and functioning of black single-parent families. *Doctoral dissertation, Howard University, 1983*. University Microfilms No. 8416946-02550.

Grollman, E. (1969). *Explaining divorce to children*. Boston: Beacon.

Grundy, S. (1987). *Curriculum: Product or praxis*. London; N.Y.: Falmer Press.

Hale, L.C. (1983). *Divorce and Single-Parent Family Counseling*. (Report No. CS-017229). Illinois State University. (ERIC Document Reproduction Service No. ED 204 000).

Hall, R.V., Axelrod, S., Tyler, L., Grief, G., Jones, F.C. & Robertson, R. (1972). Modification of behavior problems in the home with a parent observer and experimenter. *Journal of Applied Behavior Analysis, 5*, 53-64.

Hetherington, E.M., Cox, M. & Cox, R. (1978. The aftermath of divorce. In J.H. Stevens & M. Mathews (Eds.). *Mother-child-Father-child relations*. Washington, D.C.: National Association for the Education of Young Children, 149-176.

Height, D.I. (1985, March). What must be done about children having children. *Ebony*, 76-84.

Heinkel, O.A. (1974). *Priority Determination for Vocational Education Through a Formal Needs Assessment Process*. San Diego, CA: San Diego Community College. (ERIC Document Reproduction Service No. ED 086 295.

Hendricks, L. E., Howard, C. S. & Gary, L.E. (1981, March). Help-seeking behavior among urban black adults. *Journal of the National Association of Social Workers, 26*, (2), 161-164.

Hill, R. (1972). *The strengths of black families*. New York: National Urban League.

Ilfeld, F.W. (1977). Current social stressors and symptoms of depression. *American Journal of Psychiatry, 134,* 161-166.

Joyce, B.R. (1971). *Curriculum and humanistic education: Monolism vs. pluralism.* New York : Teachers College.

Juvenile crime study guages impact of drugs and family. (1988, September 19). *The New York Times.* p. 4.

Ladner, J.A. (1971). *Tomorrow's tomorrow: The black woman.* Garden City, N.Y.: Doubleday.

Lamb, J. & Lamb, W.A. (1978). *Parent education and elementary counseling.* New York: Human Sciences Press.

Landis, J.T. (1960). The trauma of children when parent's divorce. *Marriage and Family Living, 22,* 7-13.

Leavitt, S.E. & Davis, M. (1980). *Evaluating the Effectiveness of a Training Program for Single Mothers.* (Report No. CS 014902). Montreal, Canada: Proceedings of the 88th Annual Convention of the American Psychological Association. (ERIC Document Reproduction Service No. ED 197 255).

LeMasters, E. (1977). *Parents in modern America.* Homewood, IL: Dorsey.

Madsen, C.H. (1965). Positive reinforcement in toilet training of a normal child: A case report. In L.P. Ullman & L. Krasner (Eds.). *Case Studies in Behavior Modification.* New York: Holt, Rinehart & Winston.

Marsden, D. (1969). *Mothers alone: Poverty and the fatherless family.* London: Penquin.

Mayor's Management Report. (1991, September 17). New York: New York City Mayor's Office of Operations. p. 388.

McAdoo, H. P. (1981, April). *Stress and support networks of working single black mothers.* Paper presented at the Meeting of the Society for Research in Child Development, Boston, MA.

Meyer, J. (1980, Fall). Focusing on the parent in parent education. In J.D. Hartman & M.B. Markson (Eds.). Parenting in the 1980's. [Special issue]. *Journal of Children and Youth,* 8-14.

National Association of Social Workers. (1987). Helping the strong: An exploration of the needs of families headed by women. *Proceedings of the National Conference on Women's Issues, May, 1986,* (pp. 1-99). Silver Spring, MD: National Association of Social Workers.

National Council of Negro Women. (1975). *Operation Cope:Family Learning Centers for Mothers Who are Heads of Households.* Washington, D.C.: (ERIC Document Reproduction Service No. ED 116 047).

National Urban League, Inc. (1985, March). *Proceedings of the Black Family Summit.* Washington, D.C.: The National Urban League, Inc.

New York State Assembly. (1988, April). *Task force on women's issues: Summary of legislation.* Albany, N.Y.

O'Dell, S. (1974). Training parents in behavior modification: A review. *Psychological Bulletin, 81,* (7), 418-433.

Patterson, G.R., Jones, R., Whittier, J. & Wright, M.A. (1965). A behavior modification technique for a hyperactive child. *Behavior Research and Therapy, 2,* 217-226.

Pearlin, L. I. & Schooler, C. (1978, March). The structure of coping. *The Journal of Health and Social Behavior,* p.2.

Pinar, W.F. (1981). The reconceptualization of curriculum studies. In H.A. Giroux, A.N. Penna & W. Radar (Eds.). *Curriculum and Instruction.* Berkeley: McCutchan, 87-89.

Porter, L. S. (1979). *Health information and crisis prevention program for high risk families*. Presented at the 107th Annual Conference of the American Public Health Association in New York City.

Raspberry, W. (1991, October 22). Let's stop putting cartel before horse. [Opinions]. *Daily News*, p. 49.

Rodgers-Rose, L. (1980). *The black woman*. Beverly Hills: Sage.

Sarthory, J.A. (1977). Needs assessment and the practitioner: Problems and prospects. *Educational Technology, 17*, (11), 24-26.

Selltiz, J., Wrightsman, T.L. & Cook, S.W. (1981). *Research methods in social relations*. New York: Holt, Rinehart & Winston.

Srole, L., Langner, T.S., Michael, S.T., Opler, M.D. & Rennie, T.A.C. (1961). *Mental Health in the Metropolis, (Vol. 1)*. New York: McGraw-Hill.

Stack, C. (1974). *All our kin: Strategies or survival in a black community*. New York: Harper & Row.

Staples, R. (1973, July). Public policy and the changing status of black families. *The Family Coordinator*, 345-351.

Stephens, M.W. (1980, Fall). Community mental health centers' perspective on parent education. In J.D. Hartman & M.B. Markson (Eds.). Parenting in the 1980's [Special Issue]. *Journal of Children and Youth*, 16-20.

Sunley, R. (1955). Early nineteenth century American literature on childrearing. In M. Mead & M. Wolfenstein (Eds.). *Childhood in Contemporary Cultures*. Chicago: Universty of Chicago Press.

Tableman, B., Marciniak, D., Johnson, D. & Rodgers, R. (1982). Stress management training for women on public assistance. *American Journal of Community Psychology, 10*, (3), 357-367.

Tiblier, K.B. (1978). *Keeping on in New Orleans: A study of stress and coping*. Doctoral dissertation, Tulane University.

Tramontana, M.G., Sherrets, S.D. & Authier, K.J. (1980, Spring). Evaluation of parent education programs. *Journal of Clinical Child Psychology,* 40-43.

Tyler, R. (1971). *Functional education for disadvantaged youth.* New York: Committee for Economic Development.

Unruh, G.G. & Unruh, A. (1984). *Curriculum development: Problems, processes and progress.* Berkeley, CA: McCutchan.

U.S. Bureau of the Census. 1991. *Current Population Reports,* P-20, Marital Status and Living Arrangements: March 1990. Washington, D.C.: U.S. General Printing Office.

Wandersman, L.P. (1981, April 2-5). *Supportive parent education programs: What we are learning.* (Report No. PS 012228). Boston, MA: Society for Research on Child Development. (ERIC Document Reproduction Service No. 204 000).

Wandersman, L.P. (1978). Parenting groups to support the adjustment to parenthood. *Family Perspective, 12,* 117-128.

Wasserman, J. (1994, October 5). Infant death rate surges in Harlem. *Daily News*, p. 2.

Weissbourd, B. & Grimm, C. (1981, March-April). Family focus: Supporting families in the community. *Children Today,* 6-10.

Williams, M. (1990, February 27). Throwing away the gift of life. *Daily News,* p. 36.

Wilson, W.J. & Neckerman, K.M. (1985). Poverty and family structure: The widening gap between evidence and public policy issues. In S.H. Danziger & D.H. Weinberg (Eds.). *Fighting poverty: What works and what doesn't.* Cambridge, MA:Harvard University Press.

Index